THE
weeknight
DINNER
COOKBOOK

Simple Family-Friendly Recipes
for Everyday Home Cooking

Mary Younkin
creator of BarefeetInTheKitchen.com

PAGE STREET
PUBLISHING CO.

PAGE STREET
PUBLISHING CO.

First published in 2016 by

Page Street Publishing Co.

27 Congress Street, Suite 103

Salem, MA 01970

www.pagestreetpublishing.com

Distributed by Macmillan, sales in Canada by The Canadian Manda Group.

19   18   17   2   3   4   5

ISBN-13: 978-1-62414-247-5

ISBN-10: 1-62414-247-8

Library of Congress Control Number: 2016932106

Cover and book design by Page Street Publishing Co.

Photography by Mary Younkin

Printed and bound in China

Page Street is proud to be a member of 1% for the Planet. Members donate one percent of their sales to one or more of the over 1,500 environmental and sustainability charities across the globe who participate in this program.

For my boys:

Sean, Sam, Ben and Nate

Contents

Introduction

The Weeknight Dinner Cookbook is filled with recipes for tasty main dishes, flavorful side dishes and a sprinkling of sweet treats. The recipes in this book are made from scratch and categorized by the amount of time and effort required to make each dish. Cooking from scratch as simply as possible? Yes, please!

Looking for dinner in 15 minutes? Try Sweet Chipotle Chicken Bites (page 11), start to finish, on the table in barely 15 minutes. Want a slow cooker meal you can start now and have ready to eat tonight? Try Slow Cooker Mexican Pulled Pork (page 122); pile the pork into sandwiches, fill burritos with it or make a great taco salad. If you only have 5 minutes now and you need dinner in a couple of hours? Prep Chicken Parmesan Meatloaf (page 118) and dinner will be ready when you are. Whatever your occasion, there is a recipe here to help you get a great-tasting meal on the table.

You'll find notes with each recipe providing side dish ideas for each main dish. Want a delicious dinner, ready to eat in about an hour, but you only have about a few minutes' time to prep it? Try Crispy Garlic Paprika Chicken (page 114) with Cajun Roasted Potatoes (page 139) and Sweet Chili Roasted Broccoli (page 144). With just 5 additional minutes, you can make Coconut Lover's Oatmeal Bars (page 180) or Crunchy No-Bake Chocolate Peanut Butter Bars (page 168) to serve for dessert.

Cooking from scratch doesn't need to be intimidating, and it doesn't take a culinary degree to put great food on the table for your family. When I married my husband, I loved to bake, but there were only about three dinner recipes that I could cook. We ate so much spaghetti; it became a running joke in my family that it was the only thing I ever served. Despite the fact that I had little experience cooking, I loved to eat good food. And that love of eating pushed me to learn to cook and experiment in the kitchen.

As I grew more comfortable in the kitchen, I found foods that we loved and eventually had over a dozen three-ring binders filled with our favorite recipes. These were dishes that guests would request the recipes for each time they visited. I started my blog, Barefeet in the Kitchen, to share those tried-and-true favorite recipes with my family and friends. After I had shared most of our favorites, I continued cooking and sharing recipes, whether they were new or old, original creations or favorites sent to me from family, friends and blog readers.

When I began sharing recipes, I had no idea how blogging would grow to be such a huge part of my life. There are now over 1,200 recipes in the Web site archives, from breakfasts to desserts and everything in between. With so many recipes on the blog, *The Weeknight Dinner Cookbook* is designed to be a simple, easy-to-use collection of brand-new recipes along with a handful of our all-time favorites—meals that anyone can make, whether you have an hour to spend in the kitchen or just a few minutes. I've grown to love cooking, and my favorite emails to receive are the ones from people making my recipes and discovering happiness by making great food in their own kitchens.

Sharing my love of food and cooking for others are two of my favorite things. My hope is that this book brings you more joy in the kitchen and many happy meals shared with family and friends.

Mary Younkin

15-25-Minute Meals

Each recipe here will walk you through preparation to completion and provide ideas for simple sides, helping you put great-tasting meals on your table in less than 25 minutes.

Have less than 15 minutes? You can make Sweet and Saucy Broiled Chicken (page 44) with a quick homemade barbecue sauce. Roast some vegetables along with it and you'll have dinner on the table in no time. Want a dinner you can grab and go? Chicken Cordon Bleu Sliders (page 19) are my boys' favorite answer to "What do you want for dinner?" and they'd eat them every day if they could.

Cooking a truly delicious homemade meal and making it from scratch on even the busiest nights is incredibly satisfying. With a little planning and a few minutes' work, you can have a healthy, delicious meal on the table.

SWEET CHIPOTLE CHICKEN BITES

<table>
<tr><td>Yield:
4 servings</td><td>Bite-size pieces of chicken are quickly cooked in a hot skillet and then coated in a tangy, sweet and spicy glaze. Serve this chicken with rice, Simple Roasted Vegetables (page 155) or Southwest Garden Salad (page 52). This is one of the tastiest (and fastest) main dishes I make. My kids eat crazy amounts of this chicken and ask for it frequently.

This recipe is lightning fast to cook; however, cutting the chicken into ½-inch (1.3-cm) pieces does require a few extra minutes. After making this recipe countless times, I can slice the chicken and have it cooked in 15 to 20 minutes without any rushing. Allow yourself a few extra minutes initially; after you are accustomed to slicing the chicken very small, you'll find that it goes more quickly.</td></tr>
</table>

5 small boneless skinless chicken thighs, approximately 1½ lb (680 g)

1 tbsp (15 ml) light-flavored olive oil, divided

2 tsp (5 g) cornstarch or arrowroot

½ tsp kosher salt

¼ tsp smoked paprika

¼ tsp New Mexico chile powder or plain chile powder

¼ tsp cumin

¼ tsp granulated garlic or garlic powder

⅛ tsp cayenne pepper

¼ cup (60 ml) honey

1 chipotle pepper in adobo sauce, minced

1 tsp (5 ml) adobo sauce

1 tbsp (15 ml) plain white vinegar

3 green onions, very thinly sliced, for topping

Cut the chicken into ½-inch (1.3-cm) pieces and place in a medium-size bowl. Drizzle with ½ tablespoon (7.5 ml) of the oil and sprinkle with the cornstarch, salt, paprika, chile powder, cumin, garlic and cayenne. Stir or toss with your hands to coat. In a small glass measuring cup or bowl, stir together the honey, chipotle pepper, adobo sauce and vinegar.

Heat a large nonstick skillet or pan over medium-high heat. Set a plate next to the stove. Add the remaining ½ tablespoon (7.5 ml) oil to the pan. When the oil is shimmering, add the chicken and toss with tongs or stir with a spatula to coat. Continue stirring and tossing the chicken until it is no longer pink, 3 to 4 minutes. Slide the chicken onto the waiting plate and add the honey chipotle sauce to the hot skillet.

Let the sauce simmer and reduce for 1 to 2 minutes, stirring constantly. When a spatula dragged through the sauce leaves a trail, add the chicken back into the skillet. Toss with the sauce and simmer for 1 minute longer. Serve immediately, sprinkled with the green onions, or transfer back to the plate to avoid overcooking in the hot pan.

Cook's Notes: Chicken breast can be substituted for the chicken thighs. Be extra careful not to overcook the chicken breast pieces, as white meat will be less forgiving than dark meat. When the chicken has finished cooking and has been tossed with the sauce, serve immediately or remove from the hot pan. The small bites of chicken will continue to cook if left in the hot pan.

MEDITERRANEAN NACHOS

Yield:
4–5 servings

Nachos are my crew's favorite snack-style dinner food. We love them for family movie nights and for those lazy nights when no one really feels like cooking. This recipe comes together in just a few minutes, most of which are spent slicing the onion and shredding cheese.

Crunchy tortilla chips are piled high with the best of Mediterranean flavors: cheese, olives, artichoke hearts, onion and roasted red pepper. Just a few minutes in the oven is all it takes to melt the cheese. Served with hummus or sour cream, this is a meal I happily dive into every chance I get.

10 oz (280 g) tortilla chips

3 cups (360 g) mild cheddar cheese, shredded, divided

3 cups (360 g) Monterey Jack cheese, divided

1 (6-oz [170-g]) can black or kalamata olives, drained, olives sliced in half

1 (13.75-oz [385-g]) can plain or marinated artichoke hearts, drained, hearts quartered lengthwise or roughly chopped

½ small red onion, thinly sliced, about ⅓ cup (50 g)

½ cup (90 g) roasted red peppers, chopped into ½-inch (1.3-cm) pieces

¼ cup (12 g) chopped fresh Italian parsley

Plain or garlic hummus, sour cream or tzatziki sauce, for serving

Preheat the oven to 350°F (180°C, or gas mark 4). Spread about two-thirds of the tortilla chips across a large rimmed baking sheet. Combine both cheeses in a bowl and toss lightly to combine. Sprinkle about half of the cheese mixture over the chips and top with half the olives, half the artichoke hearts, half the onion and half the red peppers.

Spread the remaining one-third chips over the toppings and sprinkle with two-thirds of the remaining cheese mixture. Spread the remaining half of the toppings over the cheese and sprinkle with the remaining cheese. Bake for 6 to 8 minutes, until the cheese has melted completely. Remove from the oven and sprinkle with the parsley. Serve with hummus, sour cream or tzatziki sauce.

Cook's Notes: For a heartier meal, 1 to 2 cups (140 to 280 g) of chopped cooked chicken can be added to the layers before melting. My preference for the roasted red peppers in this recipe is a jarred variety. While I personally prefer the halved olives, feel free to save yourself a minute or two's work and substitute a 4-ounce (115-g) can of sliced olives for the whole ones.

PAN-FRIED PORK MEDALLIONS WITH CREAMY WINE SAUCE

Yield:
4 servings

The greatness of pork medallions is seen in both how quickly the pork cooks and how juicy the results are. A simple pork tenderloin is sliced into 1-inch (2.5-cm)-thick pieces (aka medallions) and then pan-fried for just a few minutes. Use the drippings in the skillet to make a creamy pan sauce and you're done. Roast some vegetables (page 155) while cooking the pork or boil some baby potatoes and you'll have dinner on the table in less than 20 minutes.

1½ lb (680 g) pork tenderloin

½ tsp kosher salt

¼ tsp freshly ground black pepper

2 tbsp (30 ml) olive oil

⅓ cup (80 ml) white wine

½ tsp chicken base

½ tsp cornstarch

Dash of paprika

½ cup (120 ml) heavy cream

2 tsp (2 g) chopped fresh Italian parsley

Slice the pork tenderloin into 1-inch (2.5-cm) medallions and lightly sprinkle each side with salt and pepper. Warm a large stainless steel skillet over medium-high heat. Add the oil and when it is shimmering, add the pork to the skillet—it is fine if the sides of the pieces touch in the skillet. Let the pork cook without touching it for 3 minutes. Set a plate next to the stove along with a piece of foil to cover the pork.

Use a metal spatula to get underneath each one and flip them over. Don't worry if they stick a bit. Cover with a lid and cook for 3 minutes. Lift each medallion with the spatula and transfer to the waiting plate; as you lift the pork, you'll see that it has browned on the edges. Cover lightly with foil to keep warm.

Place the empty skillet back on the stove over medium heat. Add the wine to the hot skillet and use a spatula to scrape up the little browned bits of meat and deglaze the pan. Add the chicken base, whisk to combine and cook for about 2 minutes. In a small cup, whisk the cornstarch and paprika into the cream until smooth. Add the cream to the saucepan slowly, whisking until combined. Continue cooking over medium heat, stirring constantly, until it thickens slightly, about 1 minute. Pour the sauce over the pork, sprinkle with the parsley and serve.

Cook's Notes: I tend to use Pinot Grigio or Chardonnay for most cooking. If you aren't a big wine drinker, the small bottles that are sold in a four-pack in most grocery stores are a great way to keep wine on hand for cooking without opening a full bottle for a recipe.

I prefer to use chicken base in lieu of chicken bouillon. The flavor is richer and it doesn't tend to be as salty. However, if you don't happen to have chicken base on hand or if you prefer bouillon, it can be substituted. You might wish to reduce the kosher salt to ¼ teaspoon; taste and adjust the salt as needed toward the end of the cooking process.

CHILI GARLIC SHRIMP

<table>
<tr><td>Yield:
3–4 servings</td><td>This dish is rich with flavor from a quick chili garlic marinade. The shrimp is cooked in a skillet or on the grill, with just enough sprinkled sugar to caramelize the outside of each shrimp as it finishes cooking. This shrimp is finger-licking good straight off the grill or out of the pan.

My family tends to crowd the stove while this is cooking and we've been known to burn our fingers with impatience to eat the shrimp out of the hot pan. Ben and Nate, my two youngest boys, will eat an entire pound of these shrimp between them and they've both chosen it as their favorite recipe in this cookbook. It's that good.</td></tr>
</table>

1 lb (455 g) large raw deveined shrimp (approximately 35 count)

MARINADE

¼ cup (60 ml) light-flavored olive oil

2 tbsp (30 ml) fresh lemon juice

2 large cloves garlic, minced

2 tsp (5 g) New Mexico chile powder or regular chile powder

1½ tbsp (18 g) sugar

½ tsp kosher salt

1 tbsp (15 ml) light-flavored olive oil

2 large cloves garlic, minced (stove top only)

1 tsp (4 g) sugar

Rinse the shrimp and lay them out on a paper towel–lined tray. Pat them dry. Remove the shells, if desired.

To make the marinade, stir together the marinade ingredients. Place the shrimp in a zip-top bag and pour the marinade over the shrimp. Remove excess air and seal. Turn the bag a few times to coat all of the shrimp and then let it rest on the counter for 15 minutes.

STOVE TOP DIRECTIONS: Heat a large stainless steel pan over medium-high heat. Add the oil and when it is hot, add the garlic. Sauté the garlic for 1 minute, sprinkle with the sugar and sauté about 30 seconds more. When the garlic is golden and fragrant, add the shrimp to the pan and discard any remaining marinade.

Spread the shrimp in a single layer across the pan and let it cook for 2 minutes. Turn the shrimp over and cook an additional 1 to 2 minutes, until pink. Increase the heat to high for 1 minute to slightly reduce any liquid. Remove from the pan when finished cooking.

GRILL DIRECTIONS: While the shrimp is marinating, soak 6 to 8 wooden skewers in water. When almost ready to grill, thread the shrimp onto the skewers. Heat the grill to medium-high and generously oil the grates to prevent the meat from sticking. Place the kabobs on the grill and sprinkle lightly with the sugar. Let cook for 3 to 4 minutes per side, turning once or twice, just until the shrimp turn pink and are cooked through.

Cook's Note: The actual cooking time for this recipe is just a few minutes. However, if you do not purchase your shrimp partially peeled and already deveined, allow at least 10 to 15 minutes to prep the shrimp before cooking.

CHICKEN CORDON BLEU SLIDERS

Yield:
6 servings

Classic chicken cordon bleu ingredients meet a handheld meal that only takes a few minutes to prepare. These sliders are stacked with chicken, ham and cheese, and a creamy honey mustard sauce ties it all together. The first time I made these sliders, my kids immediately gave them two thumbs up and asked when we could have them again. I like to serve these sliders with Mixed Green Salad with Oranges and Cranberries (page 152).

12 sweet dinner rolls

HONEY MUSTARD SAUCE
¼ cup (60 g) mayonnaise

1½ tbsp (18 g) Dijon mustard

1½ tbsp (22 ml) honey

1 tsp (5 ml) fresh lemon juice

Pinch of kosher salt

½ lb (225 g) deli black forest ham, very thinly sliced

½ lb (225 g) Swiss cheese, thinly sliced

½ lb (225 g) deli chicken breast, very thinly sliced

Preheat the oven to 400°F (200°C, or gas mark 6). Slice the dinner rolls in half and place them cut side up on a large baking tray.

To make the sauce, whisk together the sauce ingredients and spread about 1 teaspoon (5 ml) of sauce on each half.

Place a slice of ham, draped and folded into a pile, on one half of each roll. Place a half slice of cheese over the ham. Layer a slice of chicken, again draped and folded into a pile, over the cheese. Place the second half slice of cheese over the chicken. Divide any remaining cheese between the rolls and place the top roll over each slider.

Bake the sliders for 5 to 6 minutes, until the cheese has melted. Remove from the oven and serve with extra honey mustard sauce, if desired.

Cook's Note: When purchasing my meat in the deli, I ask for the meat to be sliced thin enough to fold, but not shaved and falling apart. In my experience, this is a "0.5" setting in most delis. I like the cheese in this recipe to be slightly thicker than the meat, at a "1" setting in most delis.

HUEVOS RANCHEROS BOWLS

Yield:
4 servings

My eldest son, Sam, has requested huevos rancheros for his birthday meal every year for as long as I can remember. Traditionally, huevos rancheros is a combination of eggs, potatoes and beans served over a tortilla, along with plenty of red or green chile sauce. It is delicious that way, but we've discovered that we prefer to serve ours in bowls, with the tortillas on the side. The adults scoop up bites with pieces of tortilla while the children like to fill the tortillas taco style. We make these bowls for dinner far more often than for breakfast and the whole family loves them.

1 tbsp (15 ml) olive oil

3 cups (330 g) cooked ½-inch (1.3-cm) diced potato

1 small onion, diced into ½-inch (1.3-cm) pieces, about 1 cup (160 g)

½ tsp kosher salt

¼ tsp freshly ground black pepper

1 (15.5-oz [434-g]) can pinto beans, drained and rinsed

1 cup (120 g) shredded cheddar cheese

1 cup (240 ml) red chile sauce, green chile sauce or salsa

4–8 corn or flour tortillas

2 green onions, thinly sliced

1 tbsp (14 g) butter, divided

4 eggs

2 tbsp (30 ml) water

OPTIONAL ADD-INS OR TOPPINGS

½ lb (225 g) bacon or sausage, cooked and crumbled

½ cup (80 g) diced bell pepper, sautéed with the onions

Chopped fresh tomatoes

Chopped fresh cilantro

Warm the olive oil in a large nonstick skillet over medium-high heat. Add the cooked potato, toss to coat and let them cook for 1 to 2 minutes while you dice the onion. Add the onion, sprinkle with salt and pepper and continue cooking, stirring occasionally, for about 5 minutes. While the potatoes are cooking, warm the beans on the stove or in the microwave. Set out the cheese and chile sauce. Warm the tortillas, if desired. Place the green onions in a small bowl. Transfer the potatoes to a bowl and cover loosely with foil to keep warm.

Melt ½ tablespoon (7 g) of the butter in the skillet over medium-low heat. When the butter begins to foam, tilt the pan to coat the bottom with butter. Crack 2 eggs into the skillet. When the edges of the eggs turn white, season lightly with salt and pepper. Add 1 tablespoon (15 ml) of the water to the pan and cover with a lid. Cook for 2 minutes, or until the eggs are done to your liking. Slide the cooked eggs onto a plate and tent with foil. Drain any liquid in the pan and add the remaining ½ tablespoon (7 g) butter to the hot skillet. Repeat with the remaining 2 eggs and remaining 1 tablespoon (15 ml) water.

To serve, scoop the potatoes and beans into bowls and sprinkle with cheese. Drizzle with chile sauce. Top with an egg and as many other toppings as you like. Serve with the tortillas and green onions on the side.

Cook's Notes: I use whichever cooked potatoes I happen to have on hand: leftover baked potatoes, roasted potatoes, frozen diced potatoes— pretty much any potato will work with this recipe. I roast extra potatoes almost every time I make Parmesan Herb Potatoes (page 147) or Cajun Roasted Potatoes (page 139) and they are perfect for this meal.

Any bean that you like, homemade or canned, will work in this recipe. I've used pinto, black, white, red and ranch-style beans.

BOW-TIE PASTA WITH BACON AND BRUSSELS SPROUTS

Yield: 3–4 servings	There is something amazing about the combination of Brussels sprouts and pork. Just a few strips of bacon are all it takes to give a smoky, bacon-rich flavor to this creamy sauce. Stir in the pasta and Brussels sprouts and you'll have dinner on the table in barely 20 minutes. I usually serve this as a one-dish meal, but it is also lovely with a side salad or some warm bread.

6 strips bacon, cut into ½-inch (1.3-cm)-wide strips, about ⅓ lb (150 g)

1 lb (455 g) Brussels sprouts, ends trimmed and halved

8 oz (225 g) bow-tie pasta

½ cup (120 ml) cream

¾ tsp kosher salt

½ tsp freshly ground black pepper

½ cup (56 g) shredded Asiago or Parmesan cheese (optional)

Bring a large pot of water to a boil. While the water is heating, prep the bacon and Brussels sprouts. Cook the pasta until it is tender but still a bit firm, about 12 minutes. While the pasta is cooking, warm a large skillet over medium-high heat. Add the bacon and let it cook for 2 minutes, then add the Brussels sprouts. Cook, stirring occasionally, for 8 to 10 minutes, until the bacon is cooked through and the Brussels sprouts have browned. Transfer the bacon and Brussels sprouts to a plate. Drain the grease, leaving a teaspoon (5 ml) or so of grease in the skillet.

Place the skillet back over medium-high heat. Scoop ½ cup (120 ml) of pasta water out of the boiling pasta pot and carefully pour it into the hot skillet. Use a flat spatula to scrape up the brown bits and deglaze the pan. Add the cream, salt and pepper to the skillet and stir to combine. Lower the heat to medium and let the sauce simmer for 1 to 2 minutes, until it thickens slightly. If the pasta hasn't finished cooking yet, move the sauce off the heat until the pasta finishes.

Drain the pasta well and add it to the skillet with the sauce; stir to coat well. Add the Brussels sprouts and bacon to the skillet with the pasta and stir to combine. Taste and adjust the salt, if needed. Sprinkle with the cheese before serving, if desired.

Cook's Note: Not a fan of Brussels sprouts? Feel free to substitute fresh asparagus, cut into 2-inch (5-cm) pieces, or skip the vegetables altogether. If you prefer your bacon extra crispy, you can cook it all the way to crispy and then remove it from the pan before cooking the Brussels sprouts.

SPICY GLAZED PORK WITH PEPPERS AND PINEAPPLE

Yield:
4 servings

Thin strips of pork are marinated in soy sauce and chili paste to infuse a whole lot of flavor very quickly. The pineapple balances the heat nicely without the traditional sweet flavor of a "sweet and sour" stir-fry. Stir-frying the peppers and pork takes just a few minutes and the pineapple adds just the right amount of sweetness to the dish. This stir-fry works well on its own or served over rice. I like to serve this with steamed or roasted broccoli on the side.

1 lb (455 g) thin boneless pork chops

¼ cup (60 ml) reduced-sodium soy sauce

3 tbsp (45 g) Sambal Oelek chili paste

1 tsp (4 g) sugar

2 tsp (6 g) cornstarch

1 green bell pepper, cored, seeded and sliced into ¼-inch (6-mm) strips

1 red bell pepper, cored, seeded and sliced into ¼-inch (6-mm) strips

1 tbsp (15 ml) light-flavored olive oil or refined coconut oil

1 (20-oz [910-g]) can pineapple chunks, drained well

2 green onions, thinly sliced

Cooked rice, for serving

Trim any fat from the pork chops and lay them out on the cutting board. Cover with plastic wrap and lightly pound the pork chops to about ¼ inch (6 mm) thick; thinner is fine. Slice the pork chops against the grain, into very thin strips about ¼ inch (6 mm) wide. Place the pork in a small bowl. Whisk together the soy sauce, chili paste, sugar and cornstarch. Pour the sauce over the pork and mix with your hands or stir to coat all the strips of pork. Let the pork marinate on the counter while you prep the bell peppers.

Heat the oil in a large nonstick skillet over medium-high heat. Add the bell peppers, stir and cook for 2 minutes, tossing or stirring occasionally, until slightly softened and partially browned. Add the pork and any liquid from the bowl. Cook, tossing with tongs or stirring constantly with a spatula, until the pork is white on the outside, about 2 minutes. Add the pineapple, continue stirring and cook about 2 more minutes, until the sauce is sticky and everything is well coated. Stir in the green onions and serve over rice.

Cook's Notes: Covering the meat with a sheet of plastic wrap isn't required, but it will prevent meat splatters and make cleanup easier. If you don't happen to have a meat mallet, the side of the unopened can of pineapple will work nicely for gently pounding the pork chops.

If you're unfamiliar with chili paste, you can typically find it in the Asian food section of most grocery stores. The chili paste in this recipe is countered by the sweet acidity of the pineapple. The recipe is moderately spicy as written; feel free to increase the chili paste for additional heat or reduce it slightly if your heat tolerance isn't very high.

SWEET AND SPICY SALMON WITH BROCCOLI

Salmon topped with a sweet, tangy and slightly spicy glaze is broiled for just a few minutes, resulting in a fish dinner that just might have your non-fish lovers coming back for one more bite. Drizzle a bit of glaze over the vegetables on the same pan and you'll have sweet and spicy vegetables along with the glazed salmon. If you start a pan of rice cooking on the stove as you preheat the oven, everything should be ready to eat at the same time.

1½ lb (680 g) salmon, cut into 4–5 fillets

6 tbsp (90 ml) olive oil, divided

2 tbsp (30 ml) reduced-sodium soy sauce

1½ tbsp (23 ml) apple cider vinegar

3 tbsp (45 g) apricot jam

2 cloves garlic, minced

½ tsp red pepper flakes

⅛–¼ tsp cayenne pepper

1 lb (455 g) broccoli

¾ tsp kosher salt

½ tsp freshly ground black pepper

Preheat the oven to broil on high and place a rack in the center of the oven. Line a rimmed baking sheet with foil, if you'd like, to make cleanup a breeze. Pat the salmon dry and place the salmon in the center of the rimmed baking sheet. Whisk together 4 tablespoons (60 ml) of the olive oil and the soy sauce, vinegar, jam, garlic, red pepper flakes and cayenne pepper until mostly smooth. Set aside.

Trim the broccoli into bite-size pieces. Place the broccoli in a large mixing bowl, drizzle with the remaining 2 tablespoons (30 ml) oil and sprinkle with the salt and pepper. Toss with your hands to coat well. Arrange the vegetables around the salmon on the baking tray.

Generously spoon 1 tablespoon (15 ml) of the glaze over each piece of fish. Broil for 5 minutes, remove from the oven and drizzle an additional 1 to 2 teaspoons (5 to 10 ml) glaze over each piece of salmon and lightly drizzle the broccoli with the remaining glaze. Broil for an additional 4 to 5 minutes, until the fish barely flakes apart.

Cook's Note: If your salmon fillets are larger than 4 to 6 ounces (112 to 168 g), allow an additional 1 to 3 minutes' cooking time as needed.

CRUNCHY HONEY LIME CHICKEN

Yield:
3–4 servings

Crunchy breaded chicken strips are lightly seasoned with spices, tart with lime and sweet from honey. My children absolutely love this chicken and would probably eat it every day if they could. I like to serve this with Tangy Cabbage Slaw (page 148) to balance the sweet chicken. It's also great with a simple garden salad or Cajun Roasted Potatoes (page 139).

¼ cup (30 g) all-purpose flour or brown rice flour

1 tsp (2 g) chili powder

¾ tsp kosher salt

½ tsp freshly ground black pepper

¼ tsp cayenne pepper

1 egg

2 tbsp (30 ml) milk

1 lb (455 g) boneless skinless chicken tenders

1½ cups (120 g) panko breadcrumbs, toasted if desired

2 tbsp (30 ml) olive oil (for stove top method) or cooking spray (for oven method)

2 large limes, cut into wedges

¼ cup (60 ml) honey

Whisk together the flour, chili powder, salt, pepper and cayenne in a medium-size bowl. Add the egg and milk and whisk until smooth. Add the chicken tenders to the flour mixture and stir to coat well.

Place the panko in a medium-size bowl. Set a plate next to the panko. Using your fingers or a set of tongs, dip and thoroughly coat each piece of chicken in the panko crumbs. Set the crumb-coated chicken strips on the plate.

STOVE TOP DIRECTIONS: Warm the oil in a large stainless steel skillet over medium-high heat. When the oil is shimmering, use tongs to carefully and quickly place half of the chicken in the skillet in a single layer. Let cook undisturbed for about 2 minutes, until it has lightly browned, then flip it over and cook the second side for 2 minutes.

OVEN DIRECTIONS: Preheat the oven to 425°F (220°C, or gas mark 7). Set a wire rack over a rimmed baking sheet. Lightly grease with oil. Place the crumb-coated chicken strips on the wire rack. Spray liberally with olive oil spray. Bake for 10 minutes, until the chicken is cooked through.

Set a plate next to the oven while the chicken finishes cooking. Transfer the finished chicken to the plate. Squeeze the lime wedges over the chicken and drizzle with the honey just before serving.

Cook's Note: The crumb coating on the chicken will not brown when cooking in the oven. For a more golden brown result, lightly toast the panko along with 1 tablespoon (15 ml) of oil in a skillet over medium-high heat for 2 to 3 minutes while stirring constantly. Once the panko crumbs have browned, transfer them to a bowl and begin the recipe as written above.

If chicken tenders are not available, chicken breasts can be sliced vertically into thin cutlets and then into 1-inch (2.5-cm)-wide strips.

KOREAN BEEF WITH QUICK ASIAN PICKLES

Yield:
4 servings

There is something awesome that happens when you combine tangy, cold cucumber slices with hot strips of Korean beef. Served layered over rice, stuffed into corn or flour tortillas or as a filling for lettuce wraps, this combination will work perfectly for your next taco night. This is a super-fast recipe that tastes as though you worked much harder than you really did.

1½ lb (680 g) flank or skirt steak

¼ cup (60 ml) reduced-sodium soy sauce

1 tbsp (15 g) Sambal Oelek chili paste

2 cloves garlic, minced

2 tsp (8 g) sugar

1 tsp (3 g) cornstarch

2 tsp (10 ml) olive oil, divided

6 green onions, thinly sliced, for topping

Crisp lettuce and/or small tortillas, for serving

QUICK ASIAN PICKLES
1 large English cucumber or 3 small Persian cucumbers

2 tbsp (30 ml) rice vinegar

½ tsp Sriracha hot sauce

⅛ tsp sugar

⅛ tsp salt

Slice the steak as thin as possible, taking care to slice against the grain of the meat. Aim for ⅛-inch (3-mm)-thick slices, between 2 and 3 inches (5 and 7.5 cm) long. Whisk together the soy sauce, chili paste, garlic, sugar and cornstarch in a medium-size mixing bowl. Add the beef to the mixture and let marinate on the counter for 20 minutes.

Heat 1 teaspoon (5 ml) of the olive oil in a large nonstick skillet over high heat. Add half of the beef to the skillet, toss with the oil and spread across the pan. Let the meat cook for 30 seconds, stir and spread across the pan again. Let the meat cook an additional 30 to 45 seconds and remove it to a plate. Add the remaining 1 teaspoon (5 ml) oil to the pan and repeat with the remaining meat, then add the cooked meat to the plate and sprinkle with the green onions. Set out the lettuce and/or tortillas for serving.

To make the Asian pickles, slice the cucumber as thinly as possible. Place the slices in a small bowl and add the vinegar, Sriracha, sugar and salt. Toss with tongs until well coated. Serve immediately or let the cucumbers marinate on the counter for a few minutes.

Cook's Note: If pickles aren't your thing, feel free to skip them. The beef is excellent on its own as well.

LEMON BUTTER PASTA WITH TOMATOES

Yield:
6 servings

This has been one of my favorite pasta dishes ever since I moved into my first apartment. A friend made a version of this pasta for me all those years ago and I fell head over heels for the rich buttery lemon flavor with the delicate angel hair pasta.

I often serve this with Italian Herb Chicken Bites (page 35), but this pasta stands nicely on its own. I also like to serve it with a simple salad and a loaf of warm crusty bread.

8–10 oz (225–280 g) angel hair pasta

1 recipe Italian Herb Chicken Bites (optional, page 35)

4 tbsp (56 g) butter

½ cup (80 g) minced onion

4 cloves garlic, minced

2 medium tomatoes, chopped into ½-inch (1.3-cm) pieces, about 2 cups (360 g)

¼ cup (60 ml) fresh lemon juice, about 2 lemons

1 tsp (6 g) kosher salt

½ tsp freshly ground black pepper

½ cup (60 g) freshly grated Parmesan

2 tbsp (6 g) chopped fresh Italian parsley

Cook the pasta according to the package directions. Drain and set aside. If desired, while the pasta is boiling, start cooking the Italian Herb Chicken Bites.

Melt the butter in a large nonstick skillet over medium heat. Add the onion and the garlic and sauté until fragrant and soft, about 3 minutes. Add the tomatoes, lemon juice, salt and pepper. Continue cooking for 2 minutes, until the tomatoes soften and break down a bit to make a sauce in the pan. Transfer the cooked pasta to the skillet and toss well to combine. Sprinkle with Parmesan and parsley and toss again. Serve with the chicken bites.

ITALIAN HERB CHICKEN BITES

<table>
<tr><td>Yield:
4 servings</td><td>Tender bites of chicken are tossed with Italian herbs, cooked in a drizzle of olive oil and served with a squeeze of lemon. Serve over Lemon Butter Pasta with Tomatoes (page 32) or with Italian Rice Pilaf (page 143) and a salad (dressing suggestions on pages 160–162). It's impossible to eat just a few bites of this chicken.</td></tr>
</table>

1½ lb (680 g) boneless skinless chicken thighs or breasts

3 tbsp (45 ml) olive oil, divided

1 tsp (1 g) dried oregano*

1 tsp (1 g) dried basil*

1 tsp (1 g) dried thyme*

½ tsp dried rosemary (crush long pieces)*

½ tsp dried marjoram*

½ tsp kosher salt

½ tsp freshly ground black pepper

1 lemon, cut into wedges

Cut the chicken into bite-size pieces, about ¾ inch (2 cm) in size, and place the pieces in a large mixing bowl. Drizzle with 1 tablespoon (15 ml) of the oil and sprinkle all of the herbs and spices over the chicken, rubbing them in with your hands to make sure all of the pieces are generously coated. Let rest for 10 minutes.

STOVE TOP DIRECTIONS: Heat the remaining 2 tablespoons (30 ml) oil in a very large skillet over high heat. When the oil is hot, add the chicken. Sauté, turning or stirring constantly, until the chicken is browned on the outside and cooked through, 2 to 3 minutes. Be careful not to overcook the chicken.

Remove the chicken pieces from the pan when they are finished cooking. Because the pieces are small, they will dry out if left in the hot pan. Squeeze lemon over the cooked chicken and stir.

BROILER DIRECTIONS: Preheat the oven to broil on high. Place an oven rack approximately 4 inches (10 cm) from the top of the oven. Grease a large baking sheet with about 1 tablespoon (15 ml) oil. Spread the chicken across the oiled baking sheet; press the pieces into as flat a layer as possible.

Broil the chicken for 2 minutes. Remove from the oven and stir or toss with tongs to turn the pieces. Broil for 2 more minutes. Remove from the oven and stir or toss with tongs again. Test for doneness and then repeat only if necessary. Remove from the oven, squeeze lemon over the chicken and stir. Serve warm.

Cook's Notes: My preference for this recipe is always chicken thighs, but it works well with breasts, too. The recipe can be doubled or tripled without any problems. However, if you choose to cook in a skillet rather than the oven, the chicken will need to be cooked in separate 1½-pound (680-g) batches.

A total of 4 teaspoons (4 g) Italian seasoning, homemade (page 159) or store-bought, can be substituted for the items marked with an *.

CRISPY BREADED WHITE FISH WITH SRIRACHA AIOLI

Yield:
4–6 servings

Tender flaking white fish is breaded with panko crumbs, a handful of spices and a sprinkling of fresh parsley. Sriracha aioli might sound fancy, but it's just a kicked-up mayonnaise and it makes this dish something special without much effort at all. This recipe requires barely 20 minutes from start to finish and it never fails to impress. I like to serve this fish with Buttery Garlic Green Beans (page 140) or baked potatoes (page 131) and a simple salad (dressings on pages 160–162).

1½ lb (680 g) cod or other white fish, 4–6 pieces, about ¾ inch (2 cm) thick

2 cups (230 g) panko breadcrumbs

2 tbsp (6 g) chopped fresh Italian parsley

1 tsp (6 g) kosher salt

½ tsp granulated garlic or garlic powder

½ tsp granulated onion or onion powder

½ tsp cayenne pepper (optional, skip for less heat)

¼ tsp freshly ground black pepper

2 large eggs

1 tbsp (15 ml) Sriracha hot sauce

Olive oil spray

SRIRACHA AIOLI (DIPPING SAUCE)

½ cup (120 g) mayonnaise

1 tbsp (15 ml) plain white vinegar or fresh lemon juice

1–2 tbsp (15–30 ml) Sriracha hot sauce

¼ tsp kosher salt

Preheat the oven to broil on high. Place an oven rack approximately 6 inches (15 cm) from the top of the oven. Line a large baking sheet with foil and place a metal rack over the baking sheet.

Set the fish next to the baking sheet. Combine the panko, parsley, salt, garlic, onion, cayenne and pepper in a medium-size bowl. Set the panko mixture next to the fish. Whisk together the eggs and Sriracha in a second medium-size bowl. Set the egg wash next to the crumbs. Spray or rub the wire rack with olive oil.

Press each piece of fish into the crumbs and turn to thoroughly coat. Dip the crumb-coated fish in the egg wash and then roll it through the crumbs once again. Make sure the fish is well coated with crumbs. Set the crumb-coated fish on the wire rack. Repeat with each piece of fish.

Spray the fish with olive oil cooking spray before placing in the oven. Broil for 8 to 9 minutes, until the fish is lightly browned and just cooked through.

To make the Sriracha aioli, while the fish is in the oven, whisk together the sauce ingredients. When the fish is done cooking, drizzle each serving with the aioli.

Cook's Notes: While I'm a fan of cooking with the ingredients on hand, don't skip the parsley here, as it adds an irresistible freshness to this recipe.

If you do not own a metal baking and cooling rack, you can cook the fish on the foil-lined pan. Allow an additional 3 to 4 minutes' cooking time and turn the fish over halfway through cooking. Cook the fish 2 minutes less than your estimated time, then check for doneness.

CHEESY MEXICAN PASTA

<table>
<tr><td>Yield:
8 servings</td><td>My whole family loves this cheesy, saucy, beef-filled pasta with a Southwest-inspired sauce. I especially love that it comes together in just minutes. If fresh zucchini is not in season, this recipe works well with broccoli and the cooking times will remain the same. If vegetables aren't your thing, feel free to skip them and double the pasta. This is a quick and easy dinner that keeps the whole family happy.</td></tr>
</table>

8 oz (225 g) fusilli or penne pasta

1 lb (455 g) ground beef

1 tbsp (7 g) chile powder (New Mexico chile powder, if possible)

1½ tsp (3.5 g) ground cumin*

¾ tsp kosher salt*

¾ tsp freshly ground black pepper*

½ tsp paprika, smoked or plain*

¼ tsp crushed red pepper flakes*

¼ tsp dried oregano*

¼ tsp granulated garlic or garlic powder*

¼ tsp granulated onion or onion powder*

⅛ tsp cayenne pepper (optional)*

½ tsp cornstarch

3–4 small zucchini, sliced in half lengthwise, then cut into bite-size pieces, about 4 cups (480 g)

2 (14.5-oz [406-g]) cans diced tomatoes with juices

2 cups (225 g) freshly shredded Monterey Jack cheese

2 cups (225 g) freshly shredded pepper Jack cheese

2 tbsp (6 g) chopped fresh cilantro (optional)

2 green onions, thinly sliced (optional)

Cook the pasta according to the package directions, then drain. While the pasta is cooking, brown the ground beef in a large, deep-sided skillet over medium-high heat. When the beef has almost finished cooking, sprinkle with the chile powder, cumin, salt, pepper, paprika, red pepper flakes, oregano, garlic, onion, cayenne and cornstarch.

Add the zucchini and tomatoes to the skillet with the meat. Stir and cover with a lid. Let the zucchini cook for 5 to 6 minutes and stir again. The zucchini should be fork tender, but still firm. Add the cooked pasta and the Monterey Jack cheese to the skillet (or combine everything in the bigger pasta pot, if doubling the recipe) and stir well to combine. Sprinkle with the pepper Jack cheese, remove from the heat and cover with the lid. Let the cheese melt for 3 to 5 minutes before serving. Sprinkle with the cilantro and green onions, if desired.

Cook's Notes: A total of 3 tablespoons (21 g) Mexican Seasoning Mix (page 158) or store-bought taco seasoning can be substituted for the items marked with an *.

If you prefer a one-pot meal, simply cook the pasta first and drain it. Then use the same pot for the rest of the recipe. If a shorter cooking time is your priority, two pans will reduce the cooking time by half.

This recipe can be doubled, but be warned: it will make a huge amount. I don't recommend doubling the zucchini, as it is still plenty for a double recipe. Lastly, when doubling this recipe, the cooking time will be extended by about 10 minutes and you'll want to leave the simmering pot uncovered for 2 to 3 minutes, to evaporate a bit of excess liquid, before adding the cheese.

CAPRESE SKILLET CHICKEN

Yield:
4 servings

Pan-seared chicken breasts are topped with melting mozzarella cheese, fresh tomatoes, a sprinkling of fresh basil and a drizzle of balsamic. Classic caprese is a layered salad, and this chicken mimics those layers and flavors in a simple skillet meal that everyone loves.

If you're partial to dark meat, don't let that stop you from trying this recipe. My family goes crazy over this each time it is served and, as a rule, we are not fans of chicken breasts. The chicken stays moist and juicy and the layer of cheese is irresistible. Served with a simple salad (dressing ideas on pages 160–162) or Parmesan Herb Potatoes (page 147), this meal comes together very easily.

1½ lb (680 g) chicken breasts, about 3 small

¾ tsp kosher salt, plus a pinch for finishing

¼ tsp freshly ground black pepper, plus a pinch for finishing

1 tsp (1 g) dried basil

6 oz (170 g) fresh mozzarella

2 medium-size tomatoes

8 large fresh basil leaves

2 tbsp (30 ml) olive oil

2–4 tbsp (30–60 ml) balsamic vinegar, for serving

Slice the chicken breasts in half lengthwise, making thin cutlets. If the chicken is still more than ½ inch (1.3 cm) thick, lightly pound the cutlets until they are an even ½ inch (1.3 cm) in thickness. Sprinkle the chicken with the salt, pepper and dried basil. Slice the cheese into ¼-inch (6-mm)-thick slices, slice the tomatoes into ¼-inch (6-mm)-thick slices and slice the fresh basil into thin shreds. Set on a plate next to the stove.

Warm a large stainless steel skillet over medium-high heat, add the oil and heat until shimmering. Add the chicken in a single layer across the skillet. Cook without touching for 90 seconds. Reduce the heat to medium. Flip the chicken over and top each piece of chicken with cheese and then tomato slices and cover with a lid. Cook an additional 2 to 3 minutes. The cheese should be just beginning to melt over the chicken.

Remove from the heat, uncover and test the chicken for doneness. It should be white throughout with barely a hint of pink. Sprinkle the tomatoes lightly with a pinch of salt and pepper and top with the fresh basil. Drizzle with the balsamic just before serving.

Cook's Notes: The kitchen timer is your friend for this recipe. To avoid drying out the thin pieces of chicken, watch your meat closely and set a timer for the recommended cooking times.

One teaspoon (1 g) Italian Seasoning Mix (page 159) can be substituted for the dried basil listed in the recipe. Do not skip a generous drizzle of balsamic vinegar at the end of the cooking process; it is key to the caprese flavor combination.

SPICY CHILI GARLIC BEEF AND BROCCOLI SOUP

Yield:
6–8 servings

Tender strips of beef are combined with fresh broccoli, onions, garlic and ginger in this spicy Asian soup that is my family's version of the classic Chinese beef and broccoli dish. This soup is incredibly flavorful and quite adaptable. I've made it with more broccoli and less meat, depending on what I have on hand at the time. I've also made it with ground beef for a more frugal option (see Cook's Notes).

1½ lb (680 g) flank or skirt steak

2 tbsp (16 g) cornstarch

½ tsp freshly ground black pepper, or more to taste

¼ cup (60 ml) reduced-sodium soy sauce

2 tbsp (30 ml) light-flavored olive oil, divided

1 medium yellow onion, very thinly sliced, about 1½ cups (240 g)

6 large cloves garlic, minced, about 1½ tbsp (15 g)

1-inch (2.5-cm) piece fresh ginger, minced, about 1 tbsp (6 g)

½ tsp kosher salt

8 cups (1.9 L) beef broth, hot, divided

2 large broccoli crowns, cut into bite-size florets, about 6 cups (420 g)

¼ cup (60 ml) oyster sauce

2–4 tbsp (30–60 g) Sambal Oelek chili paste

Slice the steak as thin as possible, taking care to slice against the grain of the meat. Aim for ⅛-inch (3-mm)-thick slices, between 2 and 3 inches (5 and 7.5 cm) long. Place the meat in a bowl and sprinkle with the cornstarch, pepper and soy sauce. Toss to coat. Let the meat marinate for 10 minutes while you prep the remaining ingredients.

Place a dish with a lid next to the stove. Warm 1 tablespoon (15 ml) of the oil in a large Dutch oven or soup pot over medium-high heat. When the oil is shimmering, add half of the beef to the pan. Spread across the pan and cook undisturbed for 1 minute. Stir with a metal spatula and spread across the pan again. Cook 30 to 60 seconds more, stirring occasionally. The meat should be just barely cooked through and very tender. Transfer the meat to the waiting dish and cover with the lid. Drain any extra liquid and add the remaining 1 tablespoon (15 ml) oil to the pan. Repeat with the remaining meat. Add the last of the cooked meat and any pan juices to the dish next to the stove and cover with the lid.

Add the onion, garlic, ginger, salt and ½ cup (120 ml) of the beef broth to the hot pan over medium-high heat. Stir and scrape up any brown bits from the bottom of the pan and let cook for about 3 minutes, until slightly softened and very fragrant. Add the broccoli and remaining 7½ cups (1800 ml) beef broth and increase the heat to high. When it begins to boil, stir in the oyster sauce and 2 tablespoons (30 g) of the chili paste. Taste and adjust the salt, pepper and chili paste as desired. Simmer the broccoli for about 2 minutes, until barely softened and still crisp. Remove from the heat and add the cooked beef and any juices from the dish. Stir and serve.

Cook's Notes: The chili paste provides a delicious depth of flavor. This soup can be made either mildly spicy or fiery depending on your preference. To substitute ground beef, cook and crumble the ground beef in the pot over medium heat, sprinkling it with cornstarch and pepper as it cooks. Stir the soy sauce into the beef as it finishes cooking. Leave the beef in the pot and continue with the rest of the recipe.

SWEET AND SAUCY BROILED CHICKEN

Yield:
5–6 servings

This tender chicken with a sweet and saucy barbecue-style glaze is one of my go-to dinners. Start to finish it only takes 15 to 20 minutes to get this whole meal on the table. Served with steamed veggies and extra sauce on the side for dipping, this is a meal everyone loves.

3 lb (1365 g) boneless skinless chicken thighs (about 12 small)

1 cup (240 g) ketchup

¾ cup (170 g) packed brown sugar

3 tbsp (45 ml) apple cider vinegar

1 tbsp (11 g) Dijon mustard

1 tsp (2 g) paprika

1 tsp (6 g) kosher salt

½ tsp freshly ground black pepper

¼ tsp cayenne pepper

Preheat the oven to broil on high and arrange an oven rack about 4 inches (10 cm) from the top of the oven. Line a large rimmed baking sheet with foil and place a wire rack over it. Rinse the chicken and pat dry. Combine the ketchup, brown sugar, vinegar, mustard, paprika, salt, black pepper and cayenne pepper in a mixing bowl and whisk to combine. Set aside ½ cup (120 ml) of sauce for dipping later. Place the chicken in the mixing bowl with the sauce and stir to coat, or dip each piece of chicken in the sauce to coat. Then place the chicken thighs on the prepared wire rack.

Broil the chicken on the upper rack for 8 minutes. Remove from the oven and brush generously with some of the remaining sauce in the mixing bowl. Broil 3 to 5 more minutes, until the sauce is bubbling and beginning to caramelize. Drizzle with the rest of the reserved sauce or serve the reserved barbecue sauce on the side for dipping.

Cook's Notes: If you do not have an oven-safe metal rack, you can cook the chicken directly on the rimmed baking sheet. Allow an additional 3 minutes' cooking time, if needed, and flip the chicken over about halfway through cooking. The chicken won't be quite as caramelized this way, but it's still really good.

This recipe can also be made with small boneless skinless chicken breasts or tenders. If your pieces are more than approximately ½ inch (1.3 cm) thick, pound them lightly to an even thickness. Be sure to adjust the cooking times accordingly; 3 minutes on each side is all the cooking time required for chicken tenders. If your chicken thighs are bigger than 4 ounces (112 g) each, allow 5 to 15 extra minutes' cooking time as needed.

BBQ CHICKEN AND MOZZARELLA TOSTADAS

<table>
<tr><td>

Yield:
4 servings

</td><td>

Crunchy tostadas piled with saucy barbecue chicken and gooey cheese are one of our fastest ways to get dinner on the table. My kids absolutely love this dinner, and truth be told, I love it, too. Served with a handful of raw vegetables or a quick garden salad, this is a meal that comes together in less than 15 minutes.

</td></tr>
</table>

8 tostada shells

3 cups (360 g) cooked and shredded chicken (cold is fine)

1½ cups (360 ml) barbecue sauce, homemade (pages 44 or 55) or store-bought, divided

2 cups (240 g) shredded mozzarella cheese

3 green onions, very thinly sliced

Preheat the oven to 350°F (180°C, or gas mark 4). Spread the tostada shells across two large rimmed baking sheets. Place the chicken in a small bowl and pour 1 cup (240 ml) of the barbecue sauce over it. Stir or toss with tongs to coat. Divide the chicken among the tostada shells and top generously with the cheese.

Place in the oven for 6 to 8 minutes, just until the cheese has fully melted. Remove from the oven, drizzle with the remaining ½ cup (120 ml) sauce and sprinkle with the green onions before serving.

Cook's Note: If you aren't familiar with using the slow cooker for making shredded chicken, it is beyond easy. Add 2 to 4 pounds (910 to 1820 g) of boneless skinless chicken (any combination of breasts and/or thighs works well) to your slow cooker and sprinkle with salt and pepper or any other seasonings you like. (I like to leave it simple, so that I can use the chicken in all sorts of recipes.) Cover the slow cooker and cook on low until the meat pulls apart easily with a fork. This can take from 6 to 10 hours depending on the size of your slow cooker and on how much meat you are cooking. When the meat is tender and easily shredded, use two forks or a pair of tongs to pull it apart and toss it in the juices left in the slow cooker. Transfer it to an airtight container and pour any remaining juices over it. Use this chicken for any recipe that calls for cooked or shredded chicken.

TOMATO AND HERB PASTA

Yield:
3–4 servings

Fresh herbs and a few tomatoes are at the heart of this simple pasta night. Each bowl is topped with a soft egg that provides an extra layer of creaminess; this is a meal that I can never resist. Every single bite makes my carb-loving heart so very happy.

1 tbsp (18 g) kosher salt

8 oz (225 g) thin spaghetti noodles

1 tbsp (15 ml) olive oil

2 tbsp (28 g) unsalted butter, divided

1 cup (150 g) grape tomatoes, halved

4 cloves garlic, minced

2 tbsp (6 g) chopped fresh Italian parsley

10 large basil leaves, thinly sliced

2 tsp (2 g) fresh thyme leaves

½ tsp salt, plus more for the eggs

½ tsp freshly ground black pepper, plus more for the eggs

3–4 eggs

2 tbsp (30 ml) water, divided

¼ cup (28 g) Pecorino Romano or Parmesan cheese, shredded

Bring 4 quarts (3.6 L) of water to a boil in a large pot or Dutch oven. Add the kosher salt to the water and cook the pasta according to package directions. While the pasta is cooking, prep the remaining ingredients and set next to the stove.

When the pasta has finished cooking, drain the pasta, reserving ½ cup (120 ml) of the pasta cooking water. Add the olive oil and 1 tablespoon (14 g) of the butter to the hot pan over medium heat. Add the tomatoes and garlic and cook for about 2 minutes, until warm. Add the pasta to the pan and toss with tongs to coat. Add the parsley, basil, thyme, salt and pepper. Toss with tongs and taste the pasta. Add salt, if needed. If the pasta is a little dry, add the reserved pasta water, 1 tablespoon (15 ml) at a time. Cover with a lid to keep warm.

Melt ½ tablespoon (7 g) of the butter in a large nonstick skillet over medium-low heat. When the butter begins to foam, tilt the pan to coat the bottom with butter. Add 2 eggs to the skillet. When the edges of the eggs turn white, season lightly with salt and pepper. Add 1 tablespoon (15 ml) of the water to the pan and cover with a lid. Cook for 2 minutes, or until the eggs are done to your liking. Slide the cooked eggs onto a plate and tent with foil. Drain any liquid in the pan and add the remaining ½ tablespoon (7 g) butter to the hot skillet. Repeat with the remaining 1 or 2 more eggs.

Toss the pasta add an extra tablespoon or two (15 or 30 ml) of pasta water if needed. Divide the pasta among bowls, sprinkle with the cheese and top each bowl with an egg.

Cook's Note: If poached eggs are more your style, feel free to drop a poached egg on top instead of frying the eggs. The pasta is great both ways.

CHICKEN AND ORZO SOUP

Yield:
6 servings

Tender bites of chicken are combined with orzo and tomatoes in this light soup. I typically add a can of white beans too, but they really are optional. I like the additional texture and flavor they provide, as well as the fact that they will stretch the soup for an extra serving or two. A handful of spinach and a squeeze of lime keep it fresh, while a sprinkling of Parmesan adds some depth to the flavor. Simple Italian herbs and spices complete the soup well. I like to serve this soup with a loaf of crusty bread for a super-easy weeknight meal.

1 tbsp (15 ml) olive oil

1 small yellow onion, chopped into ½-inch (1.3-cm) pieces

3 large cloves garlic, minced

⅔ cup (110 g) orzo pasta

1 lb (455 g) boneless skinless chicken thighs or breasts, chopped into ½-inch (1.3-cm) pieces

1 (15.5-oz [434-g]) can Great Northern or white beans, drained and rinsed (optional)

5 cups (1.2 L) chicken broth

1½ cups (270 g) diced fresh tomatoes or 1 (14.5-oz [406-g]) can with juices

1 tsp (1 g) dried oregano

½ tsp dried basil

½ tsp freshly ground black pepper

3–4 tbsp (45–60 ml) fresh lime juice, about 2 limes

¼ cup (28 g) freshly grated Parmesan cheese, plus more for serving

½–1 tsp (3–6 g) kosher salt, if needed

2 small handfuls baby spinach leaves (about 2 oz [56 g]), roughly chopped (optional)

Lime wedges, for serving (optional)

Warm the oil in a large pot over medium-high heat. Add the onion, garlic and orzo to the pot. Cook, stirring frequently, until the orzo is lightly browned and the skillet is fragrant, 3 to 5 minutes.

Add the chicken, beans (if desired), chicken broth, tomatoes, oregano, basil and pepper. Cover with a lid and bring to a boil and then uncover and reduce the heat to a low simmer; simmer for 12 minutes. Test the orzo and if it is almost tender, add the lime juice and Parmesan. Stir to combine and taste the broth; add salt now, only if needed. Simmer for 2 more minutes, just until the orzo is tender.

Remove from the heat and stir in the spinach leaves, if desired. They should wilt slightly, but still remain a bit firm. Serve with additional Parmesan and a wedge of lime, if desired.

Cook's Notes: Rice can be substituted for the orzo in this recipe. Same as with the orzo, the soup will be done when the rice is tender.

The chicken broth will determine how much salt is needed for this recipe. Taste the soup before adding any salt. When using store-bought broths, I rarely add more than ½ teaspoon salt to this recipe.

SOUTHWEST GARDEN SALAD
WITH CHIPOTLE LIME VINAIGRETTE

Yield:
6 servings

All the fresh vegetables in the house are combined in this salad while black beans and grilled corn make this salad filling enough for lunch or dinner. The Chipotle Lime Vinaigrette is tangy and slightly sweet, with just a tiny hint of heat from the peppers. Feel free to add an extra pepper, if you're looking for a spicy kick.

CHIPOTLE LIME VINAIGRETTE
¼ cup (60 ml) fresh lime juice

2 tbsp (30 ml) honey

2 tbsp (30 ml) light-flavored olive oil

2 tsp (8 g) minced chipotle peppers in adobo, about 1 large pepper

2 small cloves garlic, minced

½ tsp kosher salt

SALAD
1 head green leaf lettuce, chopped

1 green bell pepper, thinly sliced

1 yellow bell pepper, thinly sliced

2 carrots, julienned

1 large English cucumber, thinly sliced

1 pint (360 g) grape tomatoes, halved

1 (15.5-oz [434-g]) can black beans, drained and rinsed

2 ears grilled corn, kernels removed

1 small red onion, very thinly sliced

4 green onions, very thinly sliced

½ cup (24 g) cilantro, chopped

OPTIONAL TOPPINGS
Shredded cheese

Avocado, thinly sliced

Tortilla chips

To make the dressing, combine all the dressing ingredients in a small jar and shake to blend. Refrigerate until ready to serve.

To make the salad, in a large bowl or on a platter, combine the lettuce, bell peppers, carrots, cucumber, tomatoes, beans, corn, onions and cilantro. Add your choice of additional toppings. Drizzle with the vinaigrette and toss to coat just before serving.

Cook's Notes: The vinaigrette recipe doubles nicely and the larger recipe can easily be made in the blender. Just add the peppers whole and puree until smooth.

The salad and the dressing will keep nicely in the refrigerator for several days, making it perfect for packing into lunches as well. Store them separately and toss the salad with the dressing just before serving.

When corn is not in season, 1½ cups (195 g) frozen or canned corn can be substituted for the grilled corn. Grilled chicken or thinly sliced steak is a good addition to this salad when you want something more filling.

HONEY SRIRACHA BBQ SHRIMP

Yield:
4 servings

This sweet and spicy shrimp is perfect for a casual night at home. I barely have a chance to get it off the pan and onto our plates before the family starts eating the saucy shrimp. I like to serve this dish with Roasted Garlic Smashed Potatoes (page 151) and a simple salad (dressings on pages 160–162). Make the potatoes first and prepare the salad while the potatoes are cooking; then let the potatoes cool for a few minutes while the shrimp cooks. Serve with the reserved barbecue sauce and dip the potatoes in the sauce along with the shrimp.

1½ lb (680 g) extra-large or jumbo peeled and deveined shrimp

¾ cup (180 g) ketchup

2 tbsp (30 ml) Sriracha hot sauce

½ cup (120 ml) honey

3 tbsp (45 ml) apple cider vinegar

½ tsp kosher salt

¼ tsp cayenne pepper

Cooking oil spray

Preheat the oven to broil on high and arrange a rack approximately 4 inches (10 cm) from the top of the oven. If the shrimp are not already prepped, remove the shells but leave the tails, and devein. Rinse the shrimp, place on a paper towel–lined baking tray and pat dry. In a medium-size bowl, whisk together the ketchup, Sriracha, honey, vinegar, salt and pepper. Pour half the barbecue sauce into a small jar or bowl and do not use it for brushing the uncooked shrimp. Add the shrimp to the remaining sauce in the bowl, stir and let marinate for a few minutes.

Wipe the baking tray dry and line with foil. Place a wire rack over the baking tray and lightly spray or grease with oil. Spread the shrimp across the tray and drizzle a teaspoon (5 ml) or so of the remaining sauce from marinating over each shrimp. Broil for 2 minutes, remove from the oven and flip each shrimp over. Drizzle again with the marinade and discard any remaining marinade at this point. Broil an additional 3 to 4 minutes, until the shrimp are cooked through and the sauce is bubbling and begins to caramelize. Serve with the reserved barbecue sauce for dipping.

ALTERNATE GRILL DIRECTIONS: While the shrimp are marinating, soak 6 to 8 wooden skewers in water. When almost ready to grill, thread the shrimp onto the skewers. Heat the grill to medium-high and generously oil the grates to prevent the meat from sticking. Place the kabobs on the grill and let cook for 3 to 4 minutes per side, turning once or twice, until the shrimp turn light pink and are cooked through.

Cook's Notes: Two finely minced chipotle peppers in adobo sauce can be substituted for the Sriracha in this recipe. We love both versions. If you are unsure of the heat level in the recipe, start with half the recommended hot sauce or pepper amount.

The actual cooking time for this recipe is just a few minutes. However, if you do not purchase your shrimp partially peeled and already deveined, allow at least 10 to 15 minutes to prep the shrimp before cooking.

CREAMY KIELBASA AND BROCCOLI PASTA

Yield:
5–6 servings

Spicy kielbasa, broccoli and pasta are tossed together in a simple cream sauce to make this easy pasta dinner. My boys request this pasta more than any other and the three of them would probably eat this whole recipe, if I let them.

I love to fill our pasta dishes with plenty of vegetables, so there is almost as much broccoli in this dish as there are pasta and meat. It makes me grin to watch my son who normally dislikes broccoli eat every single saucy broccoli bite in this pasta.

8 oz (225 g) penne or fusilli pasta

1 lb (455 g) polska kielbasa sausage

1 large head broccoli

2 tbsp (30 ml) water

¾ tsp kosher salt, divided

½ cup (120 ml) heavy cream

½ tsp Italian seasoning, homemade (page 159) or store-bought

¼ tsp freshly ground black pepper

¾ cup (75 g) freshly grated Pecorino Romano or Parmesan cheese

Cook the pasta according to the package directions. Set aside about ¼ cup (60 ml) pasta cooking water and drain the pasta. While the pasta is cooking, slice the kielbasa as thin as possible, about ⅙ inch (4 mm) thick. Wash, dry and trim the broccoli into bite-size florets. Cut the broccoli stem in half lengthwise and then slice it thinly, about ¼ inch (6 mm) thick.

Place the sausage in a large, deep-sided skillet over medium-high heat. Stir and cook for 2 minutes. Add the broccoli, water and ¼ teaspoon of the salt; stir and cover with a lid. Cook for 3 minutes, stir and test for doneness. The broccoli should be bright green, fork tender and still crisp.

While the broccoli is cooking, whisk together the cream, Italian seasoning, remaining ½ teaspoon salt and pepper. Add the cooked pasta to the skillet with the sausage and broccoli. Stir and add the cream sauce. Stir again to coat thoroughly. Cook for about a minute, just to slightly thicken the sauce on the pasta. Add a tablespoon or two (15 to 30 ml) of the reserved pasta water if needed to thin the sauce. Sprinkle with the cheese and stir to melt.

Cook's Notes: If you prefer a one-pot meal, simply cook the pasta first and drain it. Then use the same pot for the rest of the recipe. If a shorter cooking time is your priority, two pans will reduce the cooking time by half.

Hard cheeses are best grated on a fine microplane. The shred will be very fine and fluffy. Pecorino Romano tends to be less expensive than Parmesan cheese, and I use the two cheeses interchangeably.

If you prefer a richer sauce, double the cream in this recipe. However, I recommend trying it as written first.

HONEY SOY BROILED SALMON

Yield:
4–5 servings

Garlic, ginger, honey and soy sauce give this salmon a huge amount of flavor with just a few minutes of marinating time. This is one of Sean's favorite salmon recipes. For the small amount of work involved, the result is impressive. Serve with jasmine rice and a garden salad (dressings on pages 160–162).

½ cup (120 ml) honey

¼ cup (60 ml) reduced-sodium soy sauce

3 large cloves garlic, minced, about 1 tbsp (10 g)

1-inch (2.5-cm) section fresh ginger, finely grated, about 1 packed tsp (2 g)

½ tsp freshly ground black pepper

2 tsp (10 ml) olive oil

1½ lb (680 g) salmon, cut into 4–5 fillets about ¾ inch (2 cm) thick

Heat the broiler on high and arrange an oven rack in the center of the oven. In a small bowl or glass measuring cup, combine the honey, soy sauce, garlic, ginger and pepper. Set aside ¼ cup (60 ml) of the sauce. Place the salmon in a gallon-size zip-top bag and pour the remaining sauce over it. Let the fish marinate on the counter for 10 to 15 minutes, and no longer than 30 minutes.

Line a rimmed baking sheet with foil and grease the foil lightly with olive oil. Place the salmon on the baking sheet and then drizzle 1 to 2 teaspoons (5 to 10 ml) of the reserved sauce on top of each piece of fish. Broil on the center oven rack just until the fish barely flakes apart with a fork, about 8 minutes. Drizzle the salmon with the reserved sauce just before serving.

Cook's Note: This can also be made with an uncut salmon fillet. Allow an additional 5 to 10 minutes' cooking time for a large piece of fish. If your salmon is thicker or thinner than noted above, simply adjust the cooking time accordingly.

EVERYTHING QUESADILLAS

Yield:
4 servings

The first time my sister Jenny made me a quesadilla, I sighed with the first bite and knew that my quesadilla-making world had been changed. For so many years, I'd been toasting my dry tortillas happily, allowing the cheese to form melted deliciousness between the layers. They are good that way—really good. However, a tortilla rubbed with just a tiny bit of butter? It's a whole different ball game. The edges and outside of the quesadilla are still crispy and that hint of butter is just perfect.

I adore quesadillas for their ability to transform leftovers into something that I crave. Chop the fillings small and fill the quesadillas with your favorite combinations. I've been known to stash leftover Slow Cooker Mexican Pulled Pork (page 122) in the back of the refrigerator, just to make a quesadilla for my lunch the following day.

8 flour tortillas

4 tsp (16 g) unsalted butter

3 cups (360 g) shredded cheese: cheddar, Monterey Jack, pepper Jack or fontina

FILLING IDEAS

Pulled pork (page 122), shredded or chopped into ½-inch (1.3-cm) pieces

Cooked chicken (page 44, 47, 114 or 126), shredded, thinly sliced or chopped into ½-inch (1.3-cm) pieces

Leftover steak, roast or brisket (page 117), sliced as thin as possible

Crumbled bacon or sausage

Roasted, steamed or lightly sautéed vegetables, chopped or sliced into ½-inch (1.3-cm) pieces

Scrambled eggs, roughly chopped

OPTIONAL TOPPINGS

Guacamole

Sour cream

Salsa

Hot sauce

*See photo on page 8 (lower left).

EVERYTHING QUESADILLAS (CONT.)

Preheat a large nonstick skillet over medium-high heat. Lightly butter a single side of one tortilla with about ½ teaspoon of butter and place it in the hot pan. Sprinkle 3 tablespoons (24 g) of cheese, ¼ cup (60 g) of your favorite filling and an additional 2 to 3 tablespoons (16 to 24 g) of cheese on just one half of the open tortilla. Fold the tortilla over on itself and let it cook for 2 to 3 minutes.

When the cheese has begun to melt and the bottom tortilla is browning slightly, flip the folded quesadilla over to cook the other side. Continue to cook until all the cheese is melted and the tortilla is crisp around the edges. Using a spatula, transfer the quesadilla to a cutting board and cut into wedges while it is hot; serve warm. Repeat as desired.

Cook's Notes: The key to this easy method for quesadillas is using a single folded tortilla, instead of stacking two tortillas. To avoid the filling spilling out when flipping, simply slide your spatula under the open side and flip the quesadilla so that the crease stays against the pan.

When making quesadillas for the whole family, I recommend using an electric griddle. Set the griddle to medium-high heat and grease the griddle with 1 tablespoon (14 g) butter. Place 3 or 4 tortillas on the griddle (leaving half of each tortilla off the side). Fill the side of the tortilla that is on the griddle, fold and follow the above directions for cooking. The quesadillas can be kept warm in a 200°F (100°C) oven on a baking tray until ready to serve.

Suggested Combinations

–Pulled pork, onions and mozzarella cheese

–Chopped chicken, peppers and pepper Jack cheese

–Chopped baby spinach, thinly sliced mushrooms, chopped chicken and fontina

–Thinly sliced apple, fontina and cheddar cheese

–Roasted broccoli and cheddar cheese

–Thinly sliced mushrooms, zucchini and Monterey Jack cheese

–Scrambled eggs, crumbled bacon or sausage and cheddar cheese

–Roasted green chile and cheddar, pepper Jack or Monterey Jack cheese

FISH TACOS WITH JALAPEÑO LIME SAUCE

Yield:
4 servings

There are countless ways to make fish tacos, and this lightning-fast method has become our favorite. It takes barely five minutes to cook the fish and the only other time involved is spent stirring together the sauce and slicing or mincing a few vegetables.

My kids (formerly fish haters) go nuts over these tacos and will happily eat as many tacos as we allow them to eat. This recipe can be doubled or tripled to feed as many people as you like. Simply wipe out the pan after each batch of fish and repeat as instructed below.

½ tsp kosher salt

½ tsp cumin

¼ tsp smoked paprika

⅛ tsp cayenne pepper

1 lb (455 g) cod or tilapia, or 4 (4-oz [112-g]) fillets

2 tbsp (30 ml) olive oil

JALAPEÑO LIME SAUCE
¼ cup (60 g) sour cream

2 tbsp (30 g) mayonnaise

1 tbsp (15 ml) fresh lime juice, about ½ large lime

1 tbsp (3 g) minced fresh cilantro

1 tsp (2 g) finely minced jalapeño

⅛ tsp kosher salt

8 (6-inch [15-cm]) white corn or flour tortillas

1 cup (70 g) finely shredded red or napa cabbage

Fresh cilantro, roughly chopped

1 large lime, cut into wedges

In a small dish, stir together the salt, cumin, paprika and pepper. Sprinkle the fish on both sides with the spice mixture. Warm the oil in a large nonstick skillet over medium-high heat. Arrange the fish across the pan and let it cook without touching it for 2 minutes. Slide a thin spatula under the fish and flip it over. Continue cooking for 2 to 3 more minutes. The fish is done when it is opaque and flakes easily with a fork. Remove the cooked fish to a plate. Use two forks to flake it apart gently, leaving plenty of bite-size pieces.

To make the sauce, while the fish is cooking, stir together the sauce ingredients and set aside. To serve, place a scoop of fish onto each tortilla. Top with the cabbage and drizzle with the sauce. Sprinkle with cilantro. Serve with the lime wedges on the side.

Cook's Note: If you have the opportunity to stir the sauce together a day in advance, the flavors will develop and meld nicely after resting overnight in the refrigerator; it's worth the effort. If the Jalapeño Lime Sauce isn't your thing, the Sriracha Aioli (page 36) is also really tasty with these fish tacos.

30–45-Minute Meals

The recipes in this chapter require a few more minutes in the kitchen, but they are all easy and delicious. In the mood for Asian flavors tonight? Ginger Chicken and Vegetable Stir-Fry (page 98) is a very flavorful dish that comes together easily, even if it's your first time making a stir-fry. Asian Chicken Pasta with Broccoli and Peppers (page 67) is another family favorite and it takes about half an hour to get on the table.

Want something with a little spicy heat and a whole lot of Mexican flavor? Cheesy Enchilada Rice Skillet (page 93) is a saucy rice dish filled with bites of chicken, black beans, chiles and plenty of cheese. My kids cheer every time I make this for dinner. Green Chile and Cheese Stuffed Chicken (page 68) will show you how to fill a chicken breast with cheese and chiles and then roll it in a pretzel crust, transforming the otherwise unexciting chicken breast into a meal that will have everyone asking for seconds.

How about a Mediterranean night? Vegetable Lover's Greek Pasta Salad (page 73) has become one of the most requested dishes I make. This salad is loaded with vegetables and it inevitably becomes a favorite for everyone who tries it. Roasted Bruschetta Potatoes (page 94) are irresistible as main dish or side.

Craving brinner for dinner? Banana Nut Pancakes (page 105) are a last-minute dinner that requires almost no advance prep. Every recipe in this chapter can be made in 30 to 45 minutes, including all prep time. Recommended side dishes are listed in the headnote of each recipe, helping you get a stress-free dinner on the table any night of the week.

ASIAN CHICKEN PASTA WITH BROCCOLI AND PEPPERS

Yield: 5–6 servings	Chunks of chicken, crisp vegetables and pasta noodles are tossed in a sticky Asian-inspired sauce that coats every single bite. My family loves this meal and when I serve it for dinner there is rarely a bite left over. I like to make this recipe on the weekend, just so I will have it for my lunches through the week. Like so many other great Chinese foods, I eat this cold straight from the refrigerator at least half the time.

8 oz (225 g) spaghetti, angel hair or linguine pasta

1½ lb (680 g) boneless skinless chicken thighs, cut into ½-inch (1.3-cm) pieces

3 cloves garlic, minced, about 1 tbsp (6 g)

2-inch (5-cm) piece fresh ginger, cut into matchsticks, about 2 tbsp (20 g)

1 tbsp (8 g) plus 1 tsp (3 g) cornstarch or arrowroot, divided

1 yellow bell pepper, cored, seeded and sliced into ¼-inch (6-mm) strips

1 red bell pepper, cored, seeded and sliced into ¼-inch (6-mm) strips

1 small head broccoli, cut into 1-inch (2.5-cm) florets, about 2 cups (140 g)

⅓ cup (80 ml) reduced-sodium soy sauce

1½ tbsp (23 g) Sambal Oelek chili paste

1½ tbsp (23 g) light brown sugar

1 tbsp (15 ml) light-flavored olive oil or refined coconut oil

3 green onions, thinly sliced, about ⅓ cup (35 g)

Cook the pasta according to package directions, drain and set aside. While the pasta is cooking, place the chicken, garlic and ginger in a medium-size mixing bowl. Sprinkle with 1 tablespoon (8 g) of the cornstarch and toss well with your hands to thoroughly coat. Set the chopped vegetables next to the stove. Stir together the soy sauce, chili paste, remaining 1 teaspoon (3 g) cornstarch and sugar. Set the soy sauce mixture next to the stove.

Heat the oil in a large, deep-sided skillet over high heat. When the oil is shimmering, add the coated chicken to the hot pan and toss the chicken pieces in the oil. Continue stirring and tossing the chicken with a metal spatula for about 3 minutes. When the chicken turns mostly white, add the vegetables and continue stirring for 2 more minutes.

Add the sauce and stir to coat the chicken and vegetables. Let everything cook for an additional 1 to 2 minutes, stirring constantly. Remove from the heat, add the cooked spaghetti noodles and toss with tongs to coat the noodles. Top with the green onions.

Cook's Notes: The key to this style of Asian stir-fry is cooking over high heat and constantly stirring and tossing the ingredients. Not including the pasta, the entire cooking time for this meal is barely 6 minutes. The only real time involved in this recipe is cooking the pasta and prepping the stir-fry ingredients.

If you do not have chili paste on hand, Sriracha hot sauce can be used.

GREEN CHILE AND CHEESE STUFFED CHICKEN

Yield:
6 servings

These tender, juicy chicken breasts are stuffed with green chiles and cheese and then coated in a cheesy pretzel crust. The first time I made this chicken it was on a whim when I ran out of panko breadcrumbs and needed to get dinner made. My eyes landed on the pretzels in the cupboard, so I tossed them in the food processor and crossed my fingers.

We all love the slightly salty, crunchy pretzel crust, and it has become a favorite new way to crust chicken. Serve this chicken with Parmesan Herb Potatoes (page 147), Simple Roasted Vegetables (page 155) or simple fresh vegetables with Ranch Dressing (page 162).

Olive oil spray

2 lb (910 g) boneless skinless chicken breasts, 6 small or 3 large, cut in half

FILLING

1⅔ cups (200 g) shredded pepper Jack cheese

½ cup (90 g) roasted green chiles, chopped, or 1 (4-oz [112-g]) can chopped green chiles

¼ tsp kosher salt

¼ tsp freshly ground black pepper

CRUST

½ cup (50 g) coarsely crushed pretzels, about 8 large pretzel rods

⅓ cup (40 g) shredded pepper Jack cheese

1 tsp (2 g) Mexican Seasoning Mix (page 158) or taco seasoning

¼ tsp kosher salt

⅛ tsp freshly ground black pepper

Preheat the oven to 400°F (200°C, or gas mark 6) and arrange an oven rack in the center of the oven. Line a rimmed baking sheet with foil and lightly spray with oil. Cut a slit in the side of each chicken breast, forming a pocket.

To make the filling, stir together the cheese, green chiles, salt and pepper in a small bowl. Stuff the filling into the chicken pockets, using all the filling. Place the stuffed chicken breasts on the greased baking sheet, pressing the edges of the chicken as closed as possible. Use toothpicks to more fully close the chicken, if desired.

To make the crust, stir together the crushed pretzels, cheese, Mexican seasoning, salt and pepper. Press the crumbs onto the top and sides of each stuffed chicken breast. Lightly spray the crumb-coated chicken with olive oil cooking spray.

Place on the center oven rack and bake for 20 to 22 minutes, until the chicken has cooked through and the crust has browned. Remove from the oven and let cool for 5 minutes before serving.

Cook's Notes: I use a food processor to coarsely crush the pretzels, but you can also do this by hand using a large zip-top freezer bag and a rolling pin. Be sure to make the crumbs as small as possible.

Some of the cheese will melt out of the chicken while it cooks, but that can be prevented by sealing the chicken closed with toothpicks, if desired. I like the sauce that the cheese creates and I simply spoon it alongside each serving.

PHILLY CHEESESTEAK POTATO SKILLET

All the flavors of a Philly cheesesteak sandwich are combined with red potatoes in this twist on the classic. Don't be intimidated by the length of this recipe at first glance! The whole meal comes together from start to finish in barely half an hour. The high heat cooks everything lightning fast. Just have all the ingredients ready to go when you start cooking and you'll be eating in no time at all.

My whole family loves this dish, and we eat it in several variations. Skip the potatoes in this recipe and serve the cheesesteak mixture stuffed into baked potatoes (page 131) or serve over rice. Stuff the meat and vegetables into sandwich rolls and then melt the cheese on top. I've also served this over crisp French fries for a fun version of cheesesteak poutine.

1¼–1½ lb (568–680 g) skirt steak or flank steak, sliced ¼ inch (6 mm) thick

3 tbsp (45 ml) reduced-sodium soy sauce

1½ tsp (9 g) kosher salt, divided

¾ tsp freshly ground black pepper, divided

¼ tsp granulated garlic or garlic powder

2 lb (910 g) red potatoes, chopped into bite-size pieces, about 6 medium-size

1 large yellow onion, sliced into ½-inch (1.3-cm) strips

1 green bell pepper, cored, seeded and sliced into ½-inch (1.3-cm) strips

1 red bell pepper, cored, seeded and sliced into ½-inch (1.3-cm) strips

8 oz (225 g) baby bella or white button mushrooms, sliced ¼ inch (6 mm) thick

2 tbsp (30 ml) olive oil, divided

8 oz (225 g) provolone cheese, very thinly sliced

Place the steak in a small bowl, add the soy sauce and sprinkle with ½ teaspoon of the salt, ¼ teaspoon of the pepper and the garlic. Stir and let the steak briefly marinate while preparing the potatoes.

Place the cut potatoes in a strainer and rinse well. Transfer to a large glass bowl, sprinkle with ½ teaspoon of the salt and ¼ teaspoon of the pepper and microwave for 6 minutes. Stir the potatoes and cook an additional 4 to 6 minutes, until fork tender. Stir again and let cool for a few minutes. (See Cook's Note for alternative oven-roasting directions.) While the potatoes are cooking, set the onion, peppers and mushrooms next to the stove.

Warm 1 tablespoon (15 ml) of the oil in a large stainless steel skillet over high heat. Add half of the steak to the skillet and spread it across the skillet in a single layer. Let the steak cook for about 30 seconds, then turn or stir with a metal spatula. Continue cooking for another minute, just until the meat has browned. Remove to a bowl and add the remaining beef to the skillet. Repeat the cooking process, adding the finished beef to the bowl. Loosely cover the bowl with foil while cooking the vegetables.

Warm the remaining 1 tablespoon (15 ml) oil in the hot skillet. Add the onion and cook, stirring occasionally, for about 3 minutes, until it begins to soften and brown on the edges. Add the peppers, sprinkle with the remaining ½ teaspoon salt and remaining ¼ teaspoon pepper and continue cooking, stirring occasionally, for about 2 minutes, until warm and still slightly crisp. Transfer the vegetables to the bowl with the steak.

PHILLY CHEESESTEAK POTATO SKILLET (CONT.)

Drain any liquid from the skillet and add the mushrooms to the hot skillet. Spread them across the pan in a single layer and let them cook undisturbed for about a minute. Stir and continue cooking until they are soft and slightly browned, about 2 minutes.

Add the cooked potatoes, steak and vegetables back into the skillet. Stir to combine and then cover with half of the sliced cheese. Stir gently to mix the cheese into the dish and begin to melt it. Repeat with the remaining slices of cheese. When the second layer of cheese has been added, cover with the lid and turn off the heat. Leave covered for a few minutes, to make sure all of the cheese is soft and melting. Serve hot.

*See photo on page 64 (upper left).

Cook's Note: Cooking the potatoes in the microwave is a great way to get this meal on the table fast. However, if you prefer to oven roast them and you have a few extra minutes, you can toss the cut potatoes with 1 tablespoon (15 ml) olive oil, sprinkle with salt and pepper and roast them on a large rimmed baking sheet at 425°F (220°C, or gas mark 7) for 30 minutes. Add the roasted potatoes to the skillet as directed above.

VEGETABLE LOVER'S GREEK PASTA SALAD

Yield:
8–10 servings

Crisp, fresh vegetables and pasta are tossed with an extra-tangy Greek dressing in this vegetable lover's salad. It's hearty enough to be the main dish for lunch or dinner. I typically make this salad for dinner and then eat the leftovers for my lunches throughout the week. This is a dish that never fails to get rave reviews. Whether it's for a potluck or a casual lunch with friends, this incredibly flavorful pasta salad steals the spotlight.

6–8 oz (168–225 g) tiny salad pasta, mini elbow or ditalini noodles

1 large English cucumber, peeled and cut into ½-inch (1.3-cm) pieces

1 small head broccoli, broken into florets and cut into ½-inch (1.3-cm) pieces

1 very small red onion, diced into ⅛–¼-inch (3–6-mm) pieces

3 cups (450 g) grape tomatoes, halved

1 yellow bell pepper, cored, seeded and chopped into ½-inch (1.3-cm) pieces

1 (6-oz [168-g]) can extra-large black olives, drained and quartered

DRESSING
½ cup (120 ml) olive oil

¼ cup (60 ml) red wine vinegar

3 tbsp (45 ml) lemon juice

4 large cloves garlic, minced

1 tbsp (2 g) dried oregano

1 tsp (6 g) kosher salt

½ tsp freshly ground pepper

½ cup (75 g) crumbled feta cheese (optional)

Cook the pasta according to package directions. Drain and rinse well to cool. While the pasta is cooking, prep the vegetables and place in a large mixing bowl.

To make the dressing, whisk together the dressing ingredients in a glass measuring cup or small bowl. Add the cooled pasta to the bowl with the vegetables and pour the dressing over the pasta and vegetables. Stir or toss well to thoroughly coat. Cover with a lid and chill in the refrigerator until ready to serve. Top with the feta, if desired, just before serving.

Cook's Note: I like to use the tiniest salad pastas possible, making it possible to have a bit of pasta and multiple vegetable flavors in each bite. You can find the packages of extra-small pasta noodles in the Hispanic food section of most grocery stores. The more common ditalini pasta also works great.

CHEESY SOUTHWEST BEEF
AND POTATO SKILLET

Yield:
4–5 servings

Ground beef, potatoes, green chiles and plenty of cheese are great ingredients on their own, but when combined in this simple 30-minute skillet meal, they create a spicy dish filled with Southwestern flavors. I like to toss in sliced zucchini for the fresh flavor and for the bright green color, but this is also tasty as a simple meat-and-potato dish if you choose to omit it.

1½ lb (680 g) medium-size red potatoes, sliced ¼ inch (6 mm) thick, about 6 cups

1½ tsp (9 g) kosher salt, divided

½ tsp freshly ground black pepper, divided

2 tbsp (30 ml) water

1½ lb (680 g) ground beef

1 tsp (3 g) ground cumin

1 tsp (3 g) chile powder

½ tsp cayenne pepper (optional)

½ tsp smoked paprika

½ tsp granulated onion or onion powder

½ tsp granulated garlic or garlic powder

1 (7-oz [196-g]) can chopped green chiles

2 medium-size zucchini, sliced ¼ inch (6 mm) thick (optional)

4 green onions, thinly sliced, about ½ cup (50 g)

1½ cups (180 g) shredded cheddar cheese

1½ cups (180 g) shredded pepper Jack cheese

2 tbsp (6 g) chopped fresh cilantro

Place the potatoes in a medium-size glass bowl. Sprinkle with ½ teaspoon of the salt and ¼ teaspoon of the black pepper, add the water and stir or toss with your hands. Microwave the potatoes for 4 minutes, stir and microwave an additional 2 to 4 minutes, until fork tender. Alternatively, you can boil the potatoes until they are fork tender, about 8 to 10 minutes, drain and then add to the skillet.

While the potatoes are cooking, crumble the ground beef into a large, deep-sided skillet and cook over medium-high heat for about 5 minutes. Sprinkle with the cumin, chile powder, cayenne, paprika, granulated onion, granulated garlic, remaining 1 teaspoon (6 g) salt and remaining ¼ teaspoon black pepper as it cooks. Drain any excess fat from the skillet, if necessary. Stir in the green chiles and cook for about 1 minute longer over medium heat. Add the softened potatoes to the skillet and stir gently to combine without breaking them up too much.

Stir in the zucchini, cover with a lid and cook for 3 minutes. Stir again, test the zucchini to see if it has begun to soften, cover and cook an additional 2 minutes, as needed. The zucchini is done when it has softened slightly and is still a bit crisp. Remove from the heat, stir in the green onions, sprinkle with the cheeses and stir again to melt. Top with the cilantro.

Cook's Notes: Fresh green chiles that have been roasted or frozen green chiles can be substituted for the canned green chiles—simply use whichever chile you have access to. Cooking the potatoes in the microwave is a great way to get this meal on the table fast.

ROASTED POTATO, SAUSAGE AND SPINACH HASH

Yield:
5–6 servings

Sausage, roasted potatoes and crisp hot vegetables are combined in this simple skillet meal that my whole family absolutely loves. Every single time I have made this for guests, they've asked for the recipe. It tastes like so much more than the sum of the ingredients. Over the past few years, this "breakfast hash" has become one of our favorite dinners. On nights when I don't really have a dinner plan, a version of this skillet is almost inevitable.

POTATOES

5 medium-size red or Yukon gold potatoes, diced into ½-inch (1.3-cm) pieces, about 3 cups (330 g)

1 tbsp (15 ml) olive oil

½ tsp kosher salt

¼ tsp freshly ground black pepper

SKILLET

1 lb (455 g) hot breakfast sausage

1 medium-size yellow onion, chopped into ½-inch (1.3-cm) pieces

2 bell peppers, any colors, cored, seeded and chopped into ½-inch (1.3-cm) pieces, about 2 cups (300 g)

¼ tsp kosher salt

¼ tsp freshly ground black pepper

4 oz (112 g) baby spinach, about 3 cups loosely packed

5–6 eggs, cooked over easy or medium (optional)

To make the potatoes, preheat the oven to 450°F (230°C, or gas mark 8). Place the potatoes on a large rimmed baking sheet and drizzle with the oil. Sprinkle with the salt and pepper and toss with your hands to coat all the potatoes. Bake for 25 to 30 minutes, until tender and barely crisp. Stir and cook an additional 10 minutes for crispy potatoes.

To make the skillet, while the potatoes are in the oven, crumble the sausage into a large skillet and cook over medium-high heat for 5 minutes. While the sausage is cooking, prep the onion and bell peppers. When the sausage is fully crumbled and mostly browned, add the onion and bell peppers to the skillet. Continue cooking for 4 to 5 minutes, until the vegetables soften slightly. Sprinkle with the salt and pepper. Stir in the potatoes and the spinach and toss to wilt the spinach a bit. Top each serving with a soft-cooked egg, if desired, just before serving.

Cook's Notes: The only real requirement with this meal is to make sure your potatoes are small, so they will cook quickly in the oven while you are preparing the rest of the ingredients. Chopping all the vegetables roughly the same size will streamline the cooking process, making it possible to cook them together and have everything done at the same time. Directions for soft cooking eggs can be found on page 48.

Hot breakfast sausage or bacon is my go-to meat for this meal. Each provides a huge amount of flavor without any effort at all. However, the beauty of this meal is that it is endlessly adaptable. If you prefer a meatless skillet, skip the meat, add a tablespoon (15 ml) of oil for cooking the vegetables and add some of your favorite canned beans at the end of the cooking. If you choose a meatless option, be sure to taste and adjust the salt and pepper to make sure it is flavorful enough.

CREAMY GREEN CHILE, CHICKEN AND SPINACH ENCHILADAS

Yield:
8 servings

Chicken and white beans are combined with a creamy green chile sauce in these enchiladas. I love adding a couple of handfuls of baby spinach to this recipe; it adds a freshness that can't be beat. However, if you aren't a fan of spinach, these enchiladas are also delicious without it.

We love to eat these enchiladas when they are still saucy and hot from the oven, along with plenty of tortilla chips for dipping. However, if you allow them to cool a bit, the enchiladas can be sliced into squares and will serve more attractively.

1 cup (240 g) sour cream

3½ cups (840 ml) green chile enchilada sauce, divided

1 (4-oz [112-g]) can chopped green chiles or ½ cup (90 g) roasted and chopped chiles

1 tsp (1 g) garlic powder

1 tsp (3 g) ground cumin

½ tsp cayenne pepper

½ tsp kosher salt

¼ tsp freshly ground black pepper

1 (15.5-oz [434-g]) can Great Northern or white kidney beans, drained and rinsed

4 oz (113 g) fresh baby spinach, roughly chopped, about 2 cups (optional)

4 cups (480 g) cooked chicken, shredded or chopped

8 white corn tortillas, cut like a pie into 6 triangles

6 cups (720 g) shredded pepper Jack or Monterey Jack cheese, divided

½ cup (24 g) chopped cilantro (optional)

Tortilla chips, for serving (optional)

Preheat the oven to 350°F (180°C, or gas mark 4). In a large mixing bowl, whisk together the sour cream and 2 cups (480 ml) of the green chile sauce until smooth. Stir in the green chiles, garlic powder, cumin, cayenne, salt and pepper. Add the beans, spinach, if desired, and shredded chicken and stir to combine.

Pour ¼ cup (60 ml) of the green chile sauce into the bottom of a 9 x 13-inch (23 x 33-cm) baking pan. Tilt to coat the bottom of the pan. Layer one-third of the tortillas across the bottom of the pan. Pour half of the chicken mixture over the tortillas. Sprinkle with 2 cups (240 g) of the cheese. Layer tortillas across the cheese layer, top with the remaining chicken mixture and sprinkle with 2 cups (240 g) of the cheese. Layer tortillas over the top. Pour the remaining 1¼ cups (300 ml) green chile sauce over the tortillas, making sure that each tortilla is coated. Sprinkle generously with the remaining 2 cups (240 g) cheese.

Bake until the cheese has completely melted and the edges of the pan are bubbling, 20 to 25 minutes. Remove from the oven and let rest for 5 to 10 minutes before serving. If desired, sprinkle with cilantro and serve with the tortilla chips for dipping.

Cook's Notes: See the note on page 47 for my favorite method for cooking chicken and shredding it for use in all kinds of recipes. Salsa verde can be substituted for the enchilada sauce in this recipe.

Traditionally, enchiladas were rolled before baking. This recipe layers the enchiladas into a dish casserole style. I've been preparing them this way since I first learned to make them and it not only is a huge time-saver but also makes it much easier to serve a crowd.

GARLICKY PEAS AND RICE WITH KIELBASA

Yield:
5–6 servings

In this simple, one-skillet meal, rice is simmered with kielbasa sausage, garlic and lots of chicken broth, infusing the rice with plenty of flavor as it cooks. The peas, green onions and parsley each add a fresh flavor that lightens this otherwise rich and hearty meal.

This is one of my boys' favorite meals. They can and will eat the entire dish on their own, if given the chance. This dish stands nicely on its own, but it also pairs well with a simple salad (dressings on pages 160–162) or Simple Roasted Vegetables (page 155).

2 tsp (10 ml) olive oil

3 cloves garlic, minced

14–16 oz (392–455 g) kielbasa sausage, sliced ¼ inch (6 mm) thick

3 cups (710 ml) chicken broth

1½ cups (248 g) jasmine rice

½ tsp granulated garlic or garlic powder

¼ tsp freshly ground black pepper

¼–½ tsp kosher salt, if needed

8 oz (225 g) frozen peas, about 1½ cups

4 green onions, sliced thin, about ½ cup (50 g)

¼ cup (12 g) chopped fresh Italian parsley

Warm the oil in a large, deep-sided skillet over high heat. Add the minced garlic and sauté, stirring, for about 1 minute, just until fragrant. Add the sausage and continue cooking, stirring frequently, for 3 minutes, until browned on the edges. Add the chicken broth, rice, granulated garlic and pepper to the pan. Stir and bring to a boil.

Reduce the heat to low, maintaining a simmer, and cover with a lid. Cook for 18 to 20 minutes, until the rice is tender and the liquid is absorbed. Remove from the heat, taste and add salt if needed. Stir in the peas, green onions and parsley. The peas will thaw and warm in just a couple of minutes.

Cook's Notes: The amount of salt needed in this recipe is determined by the chicken broth used. A low-sodium or homemade broth will possibly require a bit of additional salt. However, between the saltiness of the sausage and most store-bought chicken broths, this recipe should not require much, if any, added salt.

If you do not have jasmine rice on hand, any long-grain white rice will work for this recipe. However, my first choice is the more fragrant jasmine variety.

CHEESY RANCH CHICKEN WITH POTATO WEDGES

Yield:
4–5 servings

My family's love of ranch dressing inspired this simple dinner recipe. The herbs and spices in the dressing coat the chicken and potatoes with loads of flavor. When everything has cooked through and the potatoes are barely beginning to crisp, a layer of cheese finishes it off perfectly. Serve the chicken and potatoes with a side of ranch dressing and some sliced raw vegetables to dip alongside and dinner is served.

NOTE: The cooking time is 35 to 40 minutes, plus 6 to 12 hours' marinating time.

MARINADE

3 tbsp (45 ml) olive oil

2 tbsp (30 ml) red wine vinegar

1½ tsp (1.5 g) dried dill

1 tsp (1 g) dried chives

½ tsp dried parsley

1½ tsp (1.3 g) granulated garlic or garlic powder

¾ tsp granulated onion or onion powder

1½ tsp (9 g) kosher salt

½ tsp freshly ground black pepper

2 lb (910 g) boneless skinless chicken thighs or breasts

1½ lb (680 g) medium-size red potatoes, cut into ¼-inch (6-mm)-thick wedges

2 cups (240 g) shredded Mexican cheese blend or cheddar and Monterey Jack

2 tbsp (6 g) chopped fresh Italian parsley or cilantro

Ranch Dressing (page 162), for dipping

To make the marinade, combine all of the marinade ingredients in a gallon-size zip-top bag. Shake to blend. Add the chicken, turn to coat, place in the refrigerator and marinate for 6 to 12 hours, but no more than 24 hours.

Preheat the oven to 400°F (200°C, or gas mark 6). Place the chicken pieces on a large rimmed baking sheet. Transfer the sliced potatoes to the empty bag with the remaining marinade. Press the bag with your hands and coat the potatoes as thoroughly as possible. Transfer the potatoes to the tray with the chicken, squeezing out as much of the remaining marinade as possible. Use your hands to stir the pieces around a bit to make sure everything is coated thoroughly.

Place the pan in the center of the oven and roast for approximately 20 minutes, until the chicken is cooked through. Remove from the oven, transfer the chicken to a separate dish and loosely tent with foil to keep warm. Roast the potatoes an additional 10 to 15 minutes. Remove from the oven, add the chicken back onto the tray and sprinkle the chicken and potatoes generously with the cheese. Roast an additional 3 to 4 minutes to melt completely. Sprinkle with the parsley. Serve with the ranch dressing for dipping.

Cook's Note: If your chicken pieces are large, cut them in half and pound them to ½ inch (1.3 cm) thickness. To avoid messy splatters, place the chicken pieces in a large zip-top bag and pound them through the bag. Be sure to slice the potatoes no thicker than ¼ inch (6 mm). If the potatoes are too thick, they will not cook through in the given amount of time.

FIERY ORANGE SHRIMP PASTA

<table>
<tr><td>Yield:
3–4 servings</td><td>This is a spicy hot and garlicky shrimp pasta, with plenty of heat from the red pepper flakes in a sunshiny citrus sauce. Our favorite way to eat this shrimp is with pasta, but the dish is also delicious over steamed rice. (You'll have a good bit of extra sauce if served with rice.) Serve this with a light salad or Sweet Chili Roasted Broccoli (page 144) on the side.</td></tr>
</table>

8 oz (225 g) spaghetti or angel hair pasta

1 lb (455 g) large raw shrimp (approximately 25–28 count)

2 cups (480 ml) orange juice

⅓ cup (80 ml) white balsamic, champagne or white wine vinegar

8 large cloves garlic, minced

½–1 tsp (0.5–1 g) crushed red pepper flakes

1 tbsp (8 g) cornstarch or arrowroot

½–1 tsp (1–2 g) cayenne pepper

1 tsp (6 g) kosher salt

½ tsp freshly ground black pepper

1 tbsp (15 ml) olive oil

2 tbsp (28 g) unsalted butter, divided

2 tbsp (6 g) chopped fresh Italian parsley

Cook the pasta according to package directions, drain and set aside. While the pasta is cooking, rinse the shrimp and lay them out on a paper towel–lined tray. Pat them dry. Remove the shells, leaving the tail on each shrimp; devein if necessary. Whisk together the orange juice, vinegar, garlic, red pepper flakes, cornstarch, cayenne, salt and pepper in a small bowl or large measuring cup and set aside.

Heat a large stainless steel pan over medium-high heat. Place a plate next to the stove. Add the oil and 1 tablespoon (14 g) of the butter. When the butter has melted, add the shrimp to the pan in a single layer. Start adding the shrimp at the outside edge of the pan and work your way around and into the center, so that the shrimp in the middle of the pan, where the pan is hottest, will cook the shortest amount of time.

Begin turning the shrimp after about 60 seconds, starting with the first shrimp placed into the pan. Cook the shrimp 1 to 2 minutes longer, only until the shrimp are mostly pink. As soon as the shrimp are cooked through, remove them from the pan to the waiting plate. Add the sauce and increase the heat to high. Bring to a simmer and cook about 1 more minute, just until the sauce has thickened slightly. Swirl in the remaining 1 tablespoon (14 g) butter and then add the cooked pasta and toss until well coated. Add the shrimp back to the pasta and sprinkle with the parsley.

Cook's Notes: The actual cooking time for this recipe is 20 to 25 minutes at most. However, if you do not purchase your shrimp partially peeled and already deveined, allow 10 to 15 minutes to prep the shrimp before cooking.

I've made this recipe with both store-bought and freshly squeezed orange juice. My preference is store-bought juice, because the flavor is considerably stronger.

ITALIAN VEGETABLE SOUP

Yield:
8–10 servings

A pile of vegetables makes this simple Italian soup extra hearty; served on its own or with a loaf of warm bread, this soup has been a favorite of family and friends for as long as I can remember. Italian Vegetable Soup was the first recipe I typed up for my blog, intending just to share it with my brother. After all these years, this soup is still a constant in my freezer. The original recipe began with my mom, and over the years I've changed it according to my family's tastes. This is the soup that Sean requests the most.

1 lb (455 g) ground beef

½ small yellow onion, diced small, about ⅔ cup (110 g)

4 medium-size carrots, thinly sliced, about 2 cups (240 g)

3 stalks celery, thinly sliced, about 2 cups (240 g)

2 cups (480 ml) water

1 (14.5-oz [406-g]) can diced tomatoes with juices

1 (15-oz [40-g]) can tomato sauce

1 (15.5-oz [440-g]) can light or dark red kidney beans, drained and rinsed

1½ tbsp (23 g) beef base or beef bouillon

½ tsp dried oregano

½ tsp dried basil

½ tsp granulated garlic or garlic powder

¾ tsp kosher salt

½ tsp freshly ground black pepper

5 oz (140 g) frozen corn, about 1 cup

¼ head green cabbage, roughly chopped, about 2 cups (180 g) (optional)

Shredded Parmesan or Pecorino Romano cheese, for serving (optional)

¼ cup (12 g) chopped fresh Italian parsley, for serving (optional)

Crumble the beef into a large pot over medium-high heat, add the onion and cook for 5 to 7 minutes, until the beef has browned and the onions are slightly softened. While the beef is cooking, prep the carrots and celery. Add the carrots, celery and water to the pot. Increase the heat to high and bring to a boil as you add the tomatoes, tomato sauce, kidney beans, beef base, oregano, basil, garlic, salt and pepper. Cover with a lid. Once the soup is boiling, stir and reduce the heat slightly to avoid splattering; simmer uncovered for 15 to 20 minutes, until the carrots are tender.

Add the corn to the soup, taste the broth and adjust the salt as desired. Stir in the cabbage, if desired. Cover and simmer for a few more minutes, just until the corn is warm and the cabbage has wilted. Scoop into bowls and, if desired, sprinkle with the cheese and parsley just before serving.

Cook's Notes: This soup doubles nicely; just allow 10 to 15 additional minutes for a doubled recipe. The soup freezes well and can be reheated in the microwave straight from the freezer or allowed to thaw in the refrigerator and then reheated on the stove or in the microwave. I store the leftovers in 2-cup (480-ml) containers for easy lunches.

In the summertime, our version of this soup is typically filled with fresh vegetables instead of their canned and frozen counterparts. Fresh corn can be swapped for the frozen corn, and chopped zucchini or yellow squash can be added at the end of the cooking time along with the corn. You can make this with crumbled sausage as well or leave the meat out entirely.

CREAMY BALSAMIC SKILLET CHICKEN

This simple skillet meal is made with chicken, mushrooms and sweet onions in a creamy balsamic sauce. I serve this chicken with Tomato and Herb Pasta (page 48) or Roasted Garlic Smashed Potatoes (page 151) and Simple Roasted Vegetables (page 155). While the actual cooking time for this recipe is barely 15 minutes, allow yourself at least 20 minutes for preparing the onion, mushrooms and chicken before cooking.

1 tbsp (15 ml) olive oil

1 tbsp (14 g) butter

1 small yellow onion, very thinly sliced, about 1 cup (160 g)

2–3 cloves garlic, minced

8 oz (225 g) white button mushrooms, quartered, about 3 cups

1½ lb (680 g) boneless skinless chicken thighs or breasts, cut into 2–3-inch (5–7.5-cm) pieces

2 tbsp (16 g) all-purpose or brown rice flour

¾ tsp kosher salt, divided

½ tsp freshly ground black pepper, divided

½ cup (120 ml) chicken broth

2 tbsp (30 ml) balsamic vinegar

¼ cup (60 ml) heavy cream

1½ tsp (1.5 g) fresh thyme leaves

Warm the oil and butter in a large stainless steel skillet over medium-high heat. Add the onions and toss to coat. Cook for 4 minutes, stirring occasionally, then add the garlic and continue cooking for 1 minute, until the onions are tender and lightly browned.

While the onions are cooking, prep the mushrooms and chicken. Place the chicken pieces in a medium-size bowl. Sprinkle with the flour, ½ teaspoon of the salt and ¼ teaspoon of the pepper. Toss to coat. Alternately, place the ingredients in a large zip-top bag, seal and shake to coat.

Push the onions to the side of the skillet. Add the chicken in a single layer, leaving the onions at the side or on top of the chicken as it cooks. Cook the chicken for 3 minutes on each side, using a metal spatula to lift and turn the pieces. The chicken shouldn't be fully cooked yet, but it will be white or lightly browned all over. Transfer the chicken and onions to a plate.

Place the skillet back on the stove over medium-high heat. Add the chicken broth, balsamic vinegar, mushrooms, remaining ¼ teaspoon salt and remaining ¼ teaspoon pepper to the pan and bring to a simmer. Use a metal spatula to scrape up all the browned bits from the bottom of the pan as the mushrooms cook for 2 to 3 minutes. Add the cream, stir and transfer the chicken and onions back to the skillet. Simmer for about 3 minutes, until the chicken is cooked through and the sauce thickens slightly. Remove from the heat and stir in the fresh thyme.

Cook's Note: Our preference is chicken thighs, but this recipe also works with chicken breasts. Whether you choose to use white or dark meat, try to use smaller pieces that aren't more than ½ inch (1.3 cm) thick. If they are much thicker than that, pound them out slightly so that they will cook evenly.

ROSEMARY GARLIC ROASTED SAUSAGE WITH ONIONS AND PEPPERS

Yield:
4 servings

Rich Italian sausage, bell peppers and onions are tossed with garlic and rosemary before being roasted until tender and crisped. If you haven't tried it before, roasting onions and peppers brings out an additional sweetness that is much more flavorful than their raw or even sautéed counterparts. My eldest and youngest sons have been hooked on onions since we started roasting them this way. Served on its own or with rice, this is a huge favorite in my house.

12–16 oz (340–455 g) chicken or pork Italian sausage (4–5 links)

1 red onion, trimmed and cut into 8 wedges

1 yellow onion, trimmed and cut into 8 wedges

2 bell peppers, cored, seeded and cut into 1-inch (2.5-cm)-wide strips

3 tbsp (45 ml) olive oil

6 cloves garlic, minced

2 tbsp (6 g) minced fresh rosemary

1 tsp (6 g) kosher salt

1 tsp (2 g) freshly ground black pepper

Preheat the oven to 400°F (200°C, or gas mark 6). Place the sausage, onions and peppers on a large baking sheet. Combine the oil, garlic, rosemary, salt and pepper in a small bowl and stir to combine. Pour the oil mixture over the sausage and vegetables. Use your hands to stir the pieces around and make sure everything is well coated.

Roast for 25 to 30 minutes, until the sausage and the vegetables are hot and lightly browned on the edges.

Cook's Notes: Kielbasa or Polish sausage may be substituted for the sausage in this recipe; just cut the bigger sausage into smaller sections.

This recipe can easily be doubled. Simply use two sheet pans. Depending on how your oven cooks, you may want to rotate the pans halfway through the cooking time. Allow an additional 10 minutes' cooking time for a doubled recipe.

CHEESY ENCHILADA RICE SKILLET

Yield:
6 servings

All the flavor of creamy, cheesy, spicy chicken enchiladas is here in a quick and easy skillet meal. My kids adore Mexican food and this is one of their favorite dishes. I like to serve this skillet with tortilla chips and a tossed salad.

1 cup (165 g) white rice

2 cups (480 ml) chicken broth

4 tsp (10 g) Mexican Seasoning Mix (page 158) or taco seasoning, divided

1 large green bell pepper, cored, seeded and chopped into ½-inch (1.3-cm) pieces, about 1½ cups (225 g)

1 small yellow onion, chopped into ½-inch (1.3-cm) pieces, about 1 cup (160 g)

2 lb (910 g) boneless skinless chicken breasts or thighs, cut into ½-inch (1.3-cm) pieces

1 tbsp (15 ml) olive oil

1 (15.5-oz [434-g]) can black beans, drained and rinsed

1 (4-oz [112-g]) can chopped green chiles

½ cup (120 g) sour cream

1 cup (240 ml) green chile enchilada sauce or salsa verde

½ tsp kosher salt, if needed

2 cups (240 g) shredded Mexican cheese blend, cheddar or pepper Jack cheese

2–3 tbsp (6–9 g) chopped fresh cilantro

Combine the rice, chicken broth and 2 teaspoons (5 g) of the spice mix in a small saucepan over high heat. When the water boils, reduce to a low simmer and cover with a lid. Simmer for 18 minutes, until the rice is tender. Uncover, test the rice for doneness and fluff with a fork when done.

While the rice is cooking, prep the peppers, onions and chicken. Warm the oil in your largest skillet over medium-high heat. Add the peppers and onions to the skillet and stir to coat. Allow them to cook for about 2 minutes. Add the chicken to the skillet, sprinkle with the remaining 2 teaspoons (5 g) spice mix and continue cooking, stirring frequently, until the chicken is cooked through, about 5 minutes.

Add the beans, green chiles, sour cream and green chile sauce to the skillet. Stir to combine and bring to a low simmer. Add the cooked rice, stir again, taste and adjust the salt as desired. Sprinkle generously with the cheese. Cover with a lid and remove from the heat to allow the cheese to melt, 5 to 10 minutes. Sprinkle with the cilantro before serving.

Cook's Notes: If you don't happen to be a fan of green chiles, this recipe works quite well with red chile sauce, too. Feel free to skip the chopped green chiles or even double the amount of chiles for an extra kick.

Depending on the saltiness of the chicken broth and taco seasoning you use, you may want to add ½ teaspoon or so of salt, after tasting the final recipe, before adding the cheese.

ROASTED BRUSCHETTA POTATOES

Yield:
3 servings as
a main dish,
6 servings as
a side dish

Bruschetta is one of my favorite appetizers, and I've given it a hearty overhaul by replacing the traditional grilled bread with these roasted potatoes. Coated with olive oil, balsamic, herbs and spices, the potatoes are slightly crisp and still fluffy on the inside; the onions are sweetly caramelized on the edges and the tomatoes are bursting with rich juices. The whole house smells glorious while this is roasting. A sprinkling of cheese and fresh basil takes this right over the top, making it perfect as a light supper or as a side dish with Pan-Fried Pork Medallions with Creamy Wine Sauce (page 15) or Italian Herb Chicken Bites (page 35).

1½ lb (680 g) assorted very small red or baby Dutch potatoes, quartered

1 lb (455 g) grape or cherry tomatoes

2 yellow onions, ends trimmed and cut into 8 wedges

¼ cup (60 ml) olive oil

2 tbsp (30 ml) balsamic vinegar, plus more for serving, if desired

4 cloves garlic, minced

1 tsp (1 g) dried basil

1 tsp (1 g) dried oregano

¾ tsp dried thyme

1½ tsp (9 g) kosher salt

¾ tsp freshly ground black pepper

⅔ cup (67 g) Parmesan, finely grated (optional)

8 large basil leaves, very thinly sliced (optional)

Preheat the oven to 400°F (200°C, or gas mark 6). Place the potatoes, tomatoes and onions on a large baking sheet. In a small measuring cup, stir together the oil, vinegar, garlic, basil, oregano, thyme, salt and pepper. Drizzle the spice mixture over the potatoes and vegetables. Use your hands to stir the pieces around and make sure everything is well coated. Spread everything across the pan in a single layer.

Place the pan in the center of the oven and roast for approximately 35 minutes, until the potatoes are golden brown and fork tender. Remove from the oven and sprinkle with the Parmesan, if desired, and then place back in the oven for 2 minutes to melt the cheese. Sprinkle with the fresh basil just before serving, if desired. Serve with an additional drizzle of balsamic vinegar, if desired.

Cook's Note: This recipe can also be made with 2 pounds (910 g) Yukon gold or red potatoes, chopped into 1-inch (2.5-cm) pieces.

UN-STUFFED BELL PEPPER PASTA

<table>
<tr><td>Yield:
6–7 servings</td><td>All the flavor of classic stuffed bell peppers is packed into this quick and easy no-oven-required "stuffed bell pepper" meal. Featuring a rich and hearty beef and bell pepper sauce, this dinner comes together in barely half an hour, making it perfect for busy days. Serve this pasta on its own or with a side of warm crusty bread and/or a garden salad (dressings on pages 160–162).</td></tr>
</table>

8 oz (225 g) pasta of your choice (I recommend angel hair or rotini)

1 lb (455 g) ground beef

½ medium sweet onion, chopped into 1-inch (2.5-cm) pieces, about ½ cup (80 g)

1 yellow or orange bell pepper, cored, seeded and chopped into 1-inch (2.5-cm) pieces

1 red bell pepper, cored, seeded and chopped into 1-inch (2.5-cm) pieces

1 green bell pepper, cored, seeded and chopped into 1-inch (2.5-cm) pieces

8 oz (225 g) small fresh cremini or baby bella mushrooms, quartered

½ cup (71 g) large black olives, sliced (optional)

1 (14.5-oz [406-g]) can diced tomatoes with juices

1 (15-oz [420-g]) can tomato sauce

1 tbsp (15 ml) Worcestershire sauce

1½ tbsp (4.5 g) Italian seasoning, homemade (page 159) or store-bought

1 tsp (6 g) kosher salt

½ tsp granulated garlic or garlic powder

½ tsp freshly ground black pepper

¼–1 tsp (0.25–1 g) crushed red pepper flakes, adjusted for the desired heat level

Cook the pasta according to package directions, drain and set the empty pot back on a cool section of the stove. While the pasta is cooking, brown the ground beef in a large, deep-sided skillet. Drain, if necessary, and then add the onion and bell peppers. Cook, stirring frequently, until the vegetables begin to soften, approximately 3 minutes.

Add the mushrooms, olives, diced tomatoes, tomato sauce, Worcestershire sauce and all the spices. Stir and bring to a simmer. Reduce the heat to medium-low and continue simmering for 5 minutes. Transfer the pasta back to the empty pot and pour the sauce over the pasta. Toss with tongs or stir well to combine.

GINGER CHICKEN AND VEGETABLE STIR-FRY

Yield:
4 servings

Tender strips of chicken and crisp vegetables are tossed with a savory Asian sauce to create this super-tasty stir-fry dinner. Broccoli is one of my favorite vegetables to use in a stir-fry. The florets hold so much sauce and each bite is full of flavor. Feel free to swap out the vegetables and use your favorites. Bell peppers and snow peas also are great with this dish. If you enjoy a little heat, feel free to serve with a drizzle of Sriracha on top or add the optional chili paste to the sauce. We switch back and forth between serving this over rice and eating it on its own. The vegetables fill out the meal nicely and, for most of us, it is plenty filling without the rice.

SAUCE

3 tbsp (45 ml) oyster sauce

3 tbsp (45 ml) rice vinegar

3 tbsp (45 ml) reduced-sodium soy sauce

2 tsp (10 ml) sesame oil

1 tsp (3 g) freshly ground black pepper

1 tbsp (8 g) cornstarch

1 tbsp (15 ml) Sambal Oelek chili paste (optional)

4-inch (10-cm) piece fresh ginger, chopped into very thin matchsticks

4 large cloves garlic, minced

1 small yellow onion, sliced ¼ inch (6 mm) thick, about 1 cup (160 g)

1 bunch broccoli, cut into small florets, about 4 cups (280 g)

5 oz (140 g) button mushrooms, quartered, about 2 cups

1 tbsp (15 ml) light-flavored olive oil

4 small boneless skinless chicken thighs, cut into ¼–½-inch (6–13 mm) strips, about 1½ lb (680 g)

2 tbsp (30 ml) water

4 green onions, very thinly sliced

To make the sauce, in a small bowl or large measuring cup, whisk together the oyster sauce, rice vinegar, soy sauce, sesame oil, pepper, cornstarch and chili paste, if desired. Place the sauce mixture next to the stove.

Combine the ginger, garlic and onion in a small bowl. Combine the broccoli and mushrooms in a separate bowl and set everything next to the stove.

In a very large skillet, warm the oil over high heat. Add the chicken and cook, stirring or tossing frequently, until it has turned white and cooked mostly through, about 3 minutes. Add the ginger, garlic and onion and continue cooking while stirring constantly for 1 minute. Add the broccoli and mushrooms and cook, stirring or tossing constantly, until the pan is fragrant and the broccoli turns bright green, about 90 seconds more.

Add the water to the mixture and use a metal spatula to scrape up all the browned bits. Pour in the sauce mixture. Cook, stirring constantly, until it thickens, about 1 minute. Top with the sliced green onions before serving.

Cook's Note: The key to stress-free stir-fry recipes is prepping every single thing in advance. Make sure that every ingredient is lined up next to the stove before you even turn on the heat. The bulk of the prep time for this recipe is spent slicing and dicing the meat and vegetables, which takes about 20 minutes. Once everything is assembled and ready to cook, the actual cooking time is just a few minutes.

RED CHILE BEEF ENCHILADAS

Yield:
4–5 servings

I learned to make enchiladas from a friend's mom when I was moving into my first apartment. I loved them from the first bite. For a very long time, enchiladas were about the only thing I could reliably make. In the almost twenty years since Linda first showed me how to make her red chile enchiladas, I've made countless versions. Yet this variation on her recipe still holds a special place in my heart.

Feel free to roll them, stack them or build them however you like best. Linda served them in the New Mexican tradition, with enchiladas stacked on each plate: warm the tortilla in oil, then layer tortillas and meat sauce on the plates and finally top with cheese. I like to serve enchiladas casserole style, because they feed a crowd and there's no wait between plates. I serve these enchiladas with a salad or tortilla chips on the side.

1 lb (455 g) ground beef

½ tsp kosher salt

1 tbsp (8 g) all-purpose flour or brown rice flour

¼ cup (28 g) red chile powder

½ tsp granulated garlic or garlic powder

2 cups (480 ml) water

6 white corn tortillas, cut like a pie into 6 triangles

3 cups (360 g) pepper Jack cheese, shredded

4 green onions, thinly sliced

¼ cup (12 g) roughly chopped cilantro

FOR SERVING (OPTIONAL)
Sour cream

4–5 eggs, cooked over easy/medium or soft sunny side up

Tortilla chips

Preheat the oven to 350°F (180°C, or gas mark 4). In a large skillet over medium-high heat, cook and crumble the ground beef. Drain off any grease, sprinkle with the salt and flour and stir to coat. Whisk together the red chile powder, garlic and water. Pour into the skillet and simmer for 2 to 3 minutes.

Layer half of the tortillas across the bottom of an 8-inch (20-cm) square pan. Spoon half of the beef and red chile mixture over the tortillas and sprinkle generously with a little less than half of the cheese. Layer the remaining tortillas across the cheese, top with the remaining beef and red chile mixture and then top with the remaining cheese. Bake until the cheese has completely melted, 20 to 25 minutes.

Remove from the oven and sprinkle with green onions and cilantro. Let rest for at least 10 minutes before serving. Serve with sour cream and an egg on top, if desired, and tortilla chips on the side.

Cook's Notes: This recipe doubles nicely to fill a 9 x 13-inch (23 x 33-cm) pan. One of the best things I've learned about making enchiladas easy to slice and serve is to cut the tortillas into wedges.

If you aren't familiar with spicy Mexican foods, the sour cream helps tame the heat of the dish. While this isn't an overly spicy recipe for my family, I still like to top my serving with a scoop of sour cream.

Enchiladas are often served with a soft cooked egg on top. Personally, I love them best that way. Directions for soft cooking eggs can be found on page 48.

MAPLE DIJON GLAZED PORK TENDERLOIN

Yield: 4 servings	Sweet and savory pork tenderloin with just a hint of tang from cider vinegar is a huge favorite with all three of my kids. Using the broiler to cook tenderloin is a great way to create a nice caramelized crust with a juicy center. This is a hands-on recipe that requires a couple of bastings; however, the pork cooks in a fraction of the time required for oven roasting. I like to roast Brussels sprouts along with the pork tenderloin, but cauliflower or broccoli florets could easily be substituted. If you have a few extra minutes, the pork tenderloin works well with Roasted Garlic Smashed Potatoes (page 151) or Italian Rice Pilaf (page 143).

1½ lb (680 g) pork tenderloin

¼ tsp granulated garlic or garlic powder

¼ tsp granulated onion or onion powder

⅛ tsp kosher salt

⅛ tsp freshly ground black pepper

GLAZE

⅓ cup (80 ml) maple syrup

1½ tbsp (16 g) Dijon mustard

1½ tbsp (23 ml) apple cider vinegar

⅛ tsp kosher salt

⅛ tsp freshly ground black pepper

BRUSSELS SPROUTS

1 lb (455 g) Brussels sprouts, trimmed and halved

1 tbsp (15 ml) olive oil

¼ tsp kosher salt

¼ tsp freshly ground black pepper

Preheat the oven to broil on high and place a rack about 4 inches (10 cm) from the broiler. Line a shallow baking pan with foil and set the pork on it. Pat dry with paper towels. Sprinkle the meat very lightly on all sides with the garlic, onion, salt and pepper.

To make the glaze, combine the syrup, mustard, vinegar, salt and pepper in a small saucepan, stir to blend and bring to a boil over medium-high heat. Reduce the heat and simmer while stirring constantly, just until the glaze thickens, 2 to 3 minutes. The glaze should be slightly sticky and coat the back of a spoon. Remove from the heat. Drizzle about 2 tablespoons (30 ml) glaze over the pork and use a basting brush to coat well. Broil for 10 minutes.

To make the Brussels sprouts, while the pork is roasting, place the Brussels sprouts in a medium-size bowl and drizzle with the oil. Sprinkle with the salt and pepper and toss with your hands to coat.

Remove the pan from the oven, turn the roast over and add the Brussels sprouts around the pork on the baking pan. Drizzle the tenderloin with 2 more tablespoons (30 ml) glaze and brush again to coat the pork. (Leave a small amount of glaze in the saucepan for a final drizzle when the meat has finished cooking.) Broil for 6 more minutes, remove from the oven, check the internal temperature and broil an additional 4 to 6 minutes, if needed. When the pork reaches an internal temperature of 145°F (63°C), remove from the oven and let the meat rest for 5 to 10 minutes before slicing. Drizzle the remaining glaze over the sliced pork and the Brussels sprouts.

Cook's Note: The cooking time may vary by as much as 8 to 10 minutes, depending on the width and overall shape of the tenderloin. Cook by internal temperature, not by time. The time listed in the recipe is consistent on average, but allow yourself a few extra minutes, just in case you need them.

BANANA NUT PANCAKES

Yield:
About 20
(4-inch
[10-cm])
pancakes

Pancakes have been my go-to, I forgot to plan ahead and now "What's for dinner?" meal for as long as I can remember. Breakfast for dinner never fails to produce grins from all three of my boys. This recipe takes the average pancake and transforms it into something special with very little additional effort.

Crisp on the outside, light and fluffy on the inside, these pancakes taste like barely sweetened banana bread. Completely on their own, topped with whipped cream or smeared with peanut butter and drizzled with maple syrup, Banana Nut Pancakes are requested every time we have ripe bananas in the kitchen.

3 eggs

1 cup (240 ml) milk

1 tbsp (15 ml) vanilla extract

½ cup (112 g) packed light brown sugar

2 cups (240 g) all-purpose flour*

4 tsp (11 g) baking powder

½ tsp kosher salt

½ tsp ground cinnamon

¼ cup (60 ml) melted butter

1¼ cups (280 g) mashed banana, about 4 small ripe bananas

½ cup (55 g) chopped pecans (optional)

TOPPING OPTIONS
Fried egg

Peanut butter

Whipped cream

Butter

Maple syrup

* GLUTEN-FREE SUBSTITUTION
1½ cups (222 g) brown rice flour

⅔ cup (85 g) tapioca starch

¼ cup (44 g) potato starch

Heat an electric griddle to medium-high heat. In a large bowl, whisk together the eggs, milk and vanilla. In a separate bowl, combine the brown sugar, flour, baking powder, salt and cinnamon. Add the dry ingredients to the wet and whisk until mostly smooth. Stir in the melted butter, bananas and pecans, if desired. Pour ¼ cup (60 ml) of batter onto the griddle, leaving 1 to 2 inches (2.5 to 5 cm) between each pancake. Cook for about 3½ minutes, until deeply browned and lightly bubbled on top. Flip the pancakes and cook the second side for about 3 minutes, until golden brown. Serve immediately with any of the toppings or place in a basket lined with a tea towel to keep warm until ready to serve.

Cook's Notes: For the gluten-free recipe, allow the batter to rest for about 15 minutes prior to cooking. This will thicken the batter slightly, resulting in thicker and fluffier pancakes; the results are worth the wait.

Freezer Directions: Extra pancakes can be frozen and reheated for a delicious, quick weekday breakfast. Let the pancakes cool completely on a wire rack. Place the pancakes in a single layer in a large zip-top freezer bag. Place a sheet of parchment or wax paper over the pancakes and stack a second layer over the first; repeat as necessary. Seal tightly, removing as much air as possible from the bag. To reheat, remove from the freezer and warm the frozen pancakes in the toaster or microwave.

5—10-Minute Prep
(Meals Cook on Their Own)

This chapter is filled with hassle-free recipes for company dinners, sports nights or anytime when you just need to get your meal into the oven or slow cooker and walk away.

With a maximum of 10 minutes' hands-on time required for each of these meals, these are the recipes I make more than any other. Sheet Pan Chicken Thighs with Green Beans and Potatoes (page 109) is on our table at least once a month, if not more frequently than that. The whole family loves this meal and I especially love that it all cooks at the same time with just one pan to wash later.

Slow Cooker Mexican Pulled Pork (page 122) is one of my favorite meals to double for company dinners. I often double it just for my family; the leftover pork is even better the next day and can be used in tacos, sandwiches or stuffed into Perfect Baked, Stuffed Potatoes (page 131).

Honey Chipotle Meatloaf (page 110) is brushed with a sweet honey and spicy chipotle glaze to make the crust on this meatloaf irresistible. Served with Roasted Garlic Smashed Potatoes (page 151) and a garden salad, this is a meal perfect for Sunday dinners or casual weeknights.

SHEET PAN CHICKEN THIGHS WITH GREEN BEANS AND POTATOES

Yield:
4–5 servings

Whoever invented the sheet pan really should be given a medal. I use my half-size sheet pans at least once if not multiple times a day. Sheet pan suppers are one of my favorite ways to use them. For this easy dinner, chicken thighs, baby potatoes and fresh green beans are tossed with a simple lemon and herb vinaigrette before being roasted until tender and crisp. The chicken turns out wonderfully juicy with crisp skin every single time.

4–5 small bone-in chicken thighs, about 2 lb (910 g)

1 lb (455 g) small red potatoes, halved

1 lb (455 g) fresh green beans

¼ cup (60 ml) olive oil

2 tbsp (30 ml) fresh lemon juice

2 cloves garlic, minced

1½ tsp (9 g) kosher salt

1 tsp (1 g) dried basil*

1 tsp (1 g) dried oregano*

1 tsp (1 g) dried thyme*

½ tsp freshly ground black pepper

Preheat the oven to 400°F (200°C, or gas mark 6). Place the chicken, potatoes and green beans on a large baking sheet. In a measuring cup, stir together the olive oil, lemon juice, garlic, herbs and spices. Drizzle the mixture over the meat, potatoes and beans. Use your hands to stir the pieces around a bit and make sure everything is well coated. Be sure to leave the chicken skin side up.

Place the pan in the center of the oven and roast for approximately 50 minutes, until the chicken is golden brown and cooked through. The potatoes should be tender and slightly crisp and the green beans should be browned, crisp and somewhat shriveled.

Cook's Notes: If you have Italian seasoning, homemade (page 159) or store-bought, in your pantry, you can substitute 1 tablespoon (7 g) seasoning mix for the herbs marked with an *. If extra-crispy green beans aren't your thing, you can place the coated beans in a bowl and wait to add them for the last 15 minutes of the cooking time. Just spread them around the pan over the potatoes.

If your potatoes are bigger than about 1 inch (2.5 cm), you'll want to quarter them (instead of simply halving them) to make sure they pick up plenty of flavor from the seasonings.

HONEY CHIPOTLE MEATLOAF

Yield:
6–8 servings

This meatloaf is one of my family's favorite dinners. The sweet honey and spicy chipotle combine to make the glaze on this meatloaf irresistible. One of the things I love best about meatloaf is that it only takes a few minutes to combine all the ingredients. The meatloaf bakes mostly on its own while you have plenty of time to make a couple of side dishes. I like to serve this with Roasted Garlic Smashed Potatoes (page 151) and Sweet Chili Roasted Broccoli (page 144).

Oil, to grease the baking sheet

MEATLOAF
2 lb (910 g) ground beef

½ medium yellow onion, finely diced

2 large cloves garlic, minced

1 large chipotle pepper in adobo sauce, minced, about 1 tablespoon (9 g)

1 cup (80 g) quick oats

1 cup (240 ml) milk

1 large egg

½ tsp kosher salt

¼ tsp cayenne pepper

GLAZE
½ cup (120 ml) honey

3 chipotle peppers, minced, about 2 tablespoons (18 g)

2 tbsp (30 ml) apple cider vinegar or white wine vinegar

Preheat the oven to 350°F (180°C, or gas mark 4). Line a large baking sheet with aluminum foil and lightly grease with oil.

To make the meatloaf, combine all of the meatloaf ingredients in a large mixing bowl. Use your hands to mix thoroughly. Transfer to the lined baking sheet and shape into a loaf approximately 2 inches (5 cm) high and 4 inches (10 cm) wide, making the meatloaf as uniform in size as possible. Smooth the top and place on the middle oven rack. Bake for 60 minutes; set a timer for 30 minutes.

While the meatloaf is cooking, make the glaze by stirring together the glaze ingredients in a measuring cup. When the timer beeps at 30 minutes, remove the meatloaf from the oven and brush the glaze generously over the top. Place back in the oven and bake for 10 more minutes. Repeat the glaze twice, setting the timer for 10-minute intervals. The meatloaf is done cooking when the center temperature reaches 170°F (77°C) on a meat thermometer. The meat should have a slightly pink center. Let the meatloaf cool for 10 minutes before slicing and serving.

Cook's Notes: You can also cook the meatloaf in a traditional loaf pan, but you'll need to increase the cooking time to closer to 90 minutes. Personally, I prefer the free-form meatloaf; not only does it cook faster but it also allows more of the glaze to cover the meat's crust.

This recipe doubles nicely. We really like having leftovers for sandwiches the following day. Simply divide the meat mixture in half and form two separate meatloaves. The meatloaves can be cooked together on opposite sides of the same large baking tray.

SLOW COOKER ROSEMARY POTATO SOUP WITH HAM

Yield:
8–10 servings

Creamy potato soup is a winter favorite for almost everyone, and it is one of the easiest casual dinners I serve to guests. This is a very forgiving recipe and perfect for entertaining. It will hold in the slow cooker for up to two additional hours, an hour on low and another hour while turned off and covered with the lid.

This has been my son Ben's favorite soup ever since he was a toddler. He still asks for "the creamy white soup" and then hoards the leftovers for himself, going as far as to ask if I will double the recipe so that he can hide it in the freezer and save it just for his own lunches.

3 lb (1365 g) Yukon gold potatoes, chopped into ½-inch (1.3-cm) pieces

1 lb (455 g) cooked ham, cut into ½-inch (1.3-cm) pieces, about 3 cups

1 small yellow onion, chopped into ¼-inch (6-mm) pieces

4 cloves garlic, minced

6 cups (1440 ml) chicken broth

¼–1 tsp (6 g) kosher salt, to taste

1 tsp (1 g) dried thyme

¾ tsp ground rosemary

¼–½ tsp freshly ground black pepper, to taste

1 cup (240 ml) half-and-half or heavy cream

OPTIONAL TOPPINGS
Thinly sliced fresh chives
Finely chopped fresh Italian parsley

Combine the potatoes, ham, onion, garlic, chicken broth, salt, thyme, rosemary and pepper in the slow cooker. Stir to combine and turn the cooker onto HIGH or LOW and cover with a lid. On HIGH, it should take 3 to 4 hours for the potatoes to soften; on LOW, it should take from 6 to 8 hours.

When the potatoes are fork tender, scoop about 4 cups (960 g) of the potatoes and the ham into a blender, along with enough liquid to cover them. Blend until smooth and creamy, about a minute. Pour the thickened potato mixture back into the slow cooker along with the half-and-half. Reduce the heat to LOW. Serve immediately or let the soup simmer for an additional hour. Scoop into bowls and garnish with the optional toppings as desired.

Cook's Notes: If you happen to have leftover ham to use for this soup, that's perfect. If you do not, you can purchase uncut ham from the deli in most grocery stores. I simply ask for a pound (455 g) of ham and tell them I do not need it sliced. The saltiness of your ham and chicken broth will determine how much extra salt you'll need to add to the soup. Start with the lesser amount and add more only as needed at the end of the cooking process.

Ground rosemary is important in this recipe, because the larger dried rosemary pieces will not soften in the soup. You don't want big pieces of dried rosemary in each spoonful of creamy soup. If you prefer to use fresh rosemary, you can skip the ground rosemary and add 1 to 2 teaspoons (1 to 2 g) finely minced fresh rosemary when pureeing the soup in the blender.

CRISPY GARLIC PAPRIKA CHICKEN

Yield:
4–6 servings

Juicy, flavorful chicken with crisp skin is possible with just a drizzle of oil and a sprinkling of spices. The hardest part is waiting while the chicken cooks. My whole family loves this chicken and it's my go-to "what's for dinner?" on busy weeknights. I can typically prep this chicken and have it in the oven within five minutes. Serve this chicken with Italian Rice Pilaf (page 143) and Sweet Chili Roasted Broccoli (page 144) or Skillet Mexican Street Corn (page 136).

8–10 small bone-in chicken thighs, about 3 lb (1365 g)

1½ tsp (9 g) kosher salt

¾ tsp paprika

¾ tsp granulated garlic or garlic powder

½ tsp freshly ground black pepper

2 tbsp (30 ml) olive oil

Preheat the oven to 400°F (200°C, or gas mark 6). Line a large baking sheet with foil and place a wire rack over it. Place the chicken skin side down on the rack. Stir the spices together in a small bowl and then sprinkle half of the spices lightly over the chicken. Turn the chicken over, skin side up, drizzle with the oil and sprinkle the skin generously with the remaining spices.

Place the chicken in the center of the oven and roast for approximately 50 minutes, until the skin is crisp and golden and the chicken is cooked through. Let the chicken rest for 10 minutes before serving.

Cook's Note: I like to cook this chicken on a wire rack because it allows the grease to drain from the chicken as it cooks, resulting in extra-crispy skin. However, the rack is not required in order to make this recipe.

ALL-DAY BEEF BRISKET

<table>
<tr><td>Yield:
8–10 servings</td><td>This tender beef brisket is cooked with a heaping pile of onions and plenty of garlic. The onions and garlic will almost melt into the meat and provide rich flavor. I usually serve this with Roasted Garlic Smashed Potatoes (page 151) and Buttery Garlic Green Beans (page 140) or with Simple Roasted Vegetables (page 155).

There are two different ways to cook this brisket. The shorter length of time noted below will result in meat suitable for slicing; the longer end of that time frame will give you meat that is fork tender and falling apart, perfect for shredding.</td></tr>
</table>

4 lb (1820 g) beef brisket

½ tsp kosher salt

½ tsp freshly ground black pepper

1 tbsp (15 ml) olive oil

3 medium yellow onions, sliced into ½-inch (1.3-cm) wedges, about 4 cups (640 g)

2 cups (480 ml) beef broth

2 tbsp (30 ml) Worcestershire sauce

1 tbsp (15 ml) balsamic vinegar

6–8 large cloves garlic, minced

Warm a large heavy skillet over medium-high heat. Season the brisket all over with the salt and pepper. Add the oil to the skillet, and when it is shimmering, add the beef. Sear the meat for 3 to 4 minutes on each side, until a brown crust forms.

While the meat is cooking, prep the onions. In a large measuring cup, stir together the beef broth, Worcestershire, balsamic vinegar and garlic. Place the browned meat in the slow cooker and top with the sliced onions. Pour the broth mixture over everything.

Cover with the lid and cook on LOW for 9 to 11 hours. When the meat is done to your liking, turn the slow cooker off and let the meat rest for 15 to 20 minutes before serving.

Cook's Notes: I seldom take the time to brown meat prior to dropping it in the slow cooker. This is one time that is well worth those moments spent searing the meat.

When I have an extra minute, I like to deglaze the hot skillet with a splash of beef broth, after searing the meat. Once I've transferred the meat to the slow cooker, I pour ½ cup (120 ml) of the beef broth into the hot skillet over medium-high heat. I use a metal spatula to scrape up all the bits of browned meat and then add the skillet drippings to the other ingredients in the slow cooker.

CHICKEN PARMESAN MEATLOAF

Yield:
5–6 servings

All of the flavors in classic chicken Parmesan are amplified in this simple meatloaf. My whole family goes crazy over this dinner and every guest who has tried it agrees that it's amazing. I double this recipe almost every time I make it now, because we are sad if there are no leftovers.

If you've never bought ground chicken before, this is the perfect way to try it for the first time. This meatloaf truly tastes like chicken, but more flavorful than any chicken you've eaten in the past.

1½ lb (680 g) ground chicken, preferably thighs if possible

⅔ cup (65 g) panko breadcrumbs (gluten-free panko will work fine)

¼ cup (40 g) finely minced onion

2 tbsp (6 g) minced parsley

2 cloves garlic, minced

Zest of 1 small lemon, about 1 tsp (2 g)

2 eggs

¾ cup (75 g) shredded Pecorino Romano or Parmesan cheese

1¼ tsp (7 g) kosher salt, divided

½ tsp freshly ground black pepper

1 (14-oz [392-g]) can crushed tomatoes

½ tsp granulated garlic or garlic powder

¼ tsp crushed red pepper flakes

4–6 oz (112–170 g) mozzarella, freshly shredded

Preheat the oven to 350°F (180°C, or gas mark 4). Line a large baking sheet with aluminum foil. In a large bowl, combine the ground chicken, panko, onion, parsley, garlic, lemon zest, eggs, Pecorino Romano cheese, 1 teaspoon (6 g) of the kosher salt and pepper. Lightly mix together, using your hands or a large spoon. Transfer to the lined baking sheet and shape into a loaf approximately 2 inches (5 cm) high and 4 inches (10 cm) wide, making the loaf as uniform in size as possible. Smooth the top and place on the middle oven rack. Bake for 60 minutes, and set a timer for 30 minutes.

While the meatloaf is cooking, stir together the tomatoes, granulated garlic, red pepper flakes and remaining ¼ teaspoon salt. After the meatloaf has cooked for 30 minutes, pour ½ cup (120 ml) of the sauce over the top and spread gently to coat. Bake for another 15 minutes, then repeat with the sauce and sprinkle with the mozzarella.

Bake until the cheese has completely melted, 6 to 8 minutes. The meatloaf is done cooking when the center temperature reaches 160°F (71°C) on a meat thermometer. It should be mostly white when it has finished cooking. Let the meatloaf cool for 10 minutes before slicing and serving.

Cook's Notes: This is the only recipe I'm including in the book that pushes the limits of the chapter's time frame. You will likely have around 15 minutes of hands-on time for this meatloaf, but I promise you it is worth it. I simply couldn't exclude this recipe. You'll agree after your very first bite.

Fresh mozzarella is a fairly soft cheese, and as a result, it will be much easier to shred if you place it in the freezer for 5 to 10 minutes before shredding it.

See the Cook's Note on page 110 for directions on doubling a meatloaf recipe.

CAJUN-RUBBED CHICKEN OR PORK CHOPS

Yield:
4 servings

Cajun herbs and spices are rubbed onto chicken or thick-cut pork chops, creating a whole lot of flavor along with a crisp crust surrounding the meat. Thick-cut pork chops have forever changed my opinion of pork chops because they are reminiscent of steaks at a fraction of the cost. The bone-in chicken thighs are my first preference for this rub. We roast or grill chicken this way at least once a month.

1½ tsp (3.5 g) smoked or plain paprika

1½ tsp (3 g) granulated garlic or garlic powder

1 tsp (6 g) kosher salt

1 tsp (2 g) freshly ground black pepper

1 tsp (2 g) granulated onion or onion powder

1 tsp (1 g) dried oregano

¾ tsp dried thyme

½ tsp cayenne pepper

3 tbsp (45 ml) olive oil

1½ lb (680 g) boneless skinless chicken thighs or breasts OR bone-in skin-on chicken thighs OR thick-cut boneless pork chops, 1–1¼ inches (2.5–3.1 cm) thick

In a small bowl, stir together the herbs and spices with the oil. Let the spice mixture sit for 5 minutes while it forms a paste-like consistency. Rub the spice mixture all over both sides of each piece of chicken or pork chop.

BROILING DIRECTIONS (for boneless meat only): Preheat the oven to broil on high. Position an oven rack approximately 4 inches (10 cm) from the broiler. Line a large baking sheet with foil. Arrange the meat on the baking sheet. Broil for 6 minutes, turn over and broil for 4 to 8 minutes, until cooked through but not at all dry. Let rest for 5 minutes before serving.

ROASTING DIRECTIONS: Preheat the oven to 350°F (180°C, or gas mark 4) for boneless meat or 400°F (200°C, or gas mark 6) for bone-in chicken thighs. Line a large baking sheet with foil. Arrange the meat on the baking sheet. Roast boneless meat for 20 to 24 minutes, until cooked through but not at all dry. Roast bone-in chicken thighs for 1 hour. Let rest for 5 minutes before serving.

GRILLING DIRECTIONS: Preheat the grill to medium-high, 450°F to 500°F (232°C to 260°C). You're going to use an indirect cooking method, so either heat the center of the grill and plan to cook at the sides or heat the sides and plan to cook in the center of the grill. Lightly grease or spray the grates with oil. Arrange the meat on the grill and close the lid. Cook pork chops for 28 to 33 minutes, turning once. Cook boneless skinless thighs and breasts for 12 to 16 minutes, turning once. Cook bone-in thighs (skin side up) for 45 to 50 minutes, then turn over and cook for 5 to 10 more minutes, until the skin is crisp and golden brown. Let rest for 5 minutes before serving.

Cook's Note: While a meat thermometer isn't required for this recipe, I recommend one. I pull my pork from the heat at 145°F (63°C); the temperature of the meat will continue to rise for a few minutes while it is resting at room temperature. The cooking time will vary according to the size of each individual piece of meat, especially when grilling.

SLOW COOKER MEXICAN PULLED PORK

Yield:
8–10 servings

This pork roast is generously rubbed with Mexican herbs and spices before being slowly cooked until it's almost falling apart. The slow cooker does all the work and turns the simple pork into some of the most flavorful meat you can imagine.

Stuffed into tacos, sandwiches or baked potatoes, served alongside rice or mashed potatoes, this Mexican pulled pork works well for any occasion. This is an awesome recipe to have in your pocket and a great reason to keep a pork roast in the freezer.

4 lb (1820 g) pork roast, shoulder, butt or picnic cut

1 tbsp (7 g) chile powder, New Mexico chile powder if possible

2 tsp (2 g) dried oregano

2 tsp (2 g) granulated garlic or garlic powder

1½ tsp (3.5 g) smoked or regular paprika

1½ tsp (3.5 g) ground cumin

1½ tsp (9 g) kosher salt

1 tsp (1 g) granulated onion or onion powder

½ tsp cayenne pepper

⅓ cup (80 ml) orange juice

⅔ cup (160 ml) water

Lime wedges, for serving (optional)

Rinse and pat dry the pork roast. Stir together the chile powder, oregano, garlic, paprika, cumin, salt, onion and cayenne in a small bowl. Rub the herbs and spices all over the pork roast. Place the roast in the slow cooker with the fat cap facing up. Pour the orange juice and water over the roast.

Cover with the lid and cook on LOW for 10 to 11 hours, until the pork is tender and falling apart. (If the fat cap is still intact over the roast, pull the biggest pieces of it off and discard.) Pull the roast apart with tongs or two forks. Shred it gently, leaving plenty of bite-size pieces. Toss the pork in any juices left in the bottom of the pot. Serve with a wedge of lime to squeeze over the meat, if desired.

Cook's Notes: Shoulder, butt and picnic cut pork roasts work best for this recipe. Bone-in or boneless roasts will work fine. This recipe doubles very nicely with an 8- to 9-pound (3640- to 4095-g) roast and doesn't require much additional cooking time.

Leftover pork will keep nicely in the refrigerator or the freezer. Pour any remaining juices over the shredded pork before refrigerating or freezing. Thaw and reheat in the microwave or on the stove.

For crispy carnitas-style pork, spread about 2 cups (240 g) of the cooked pork in a nonstick skillet over medium-high heat. Press it flat and let it cook for about 2 minutes, until browned and most of the juices have been absorbed. Stir or flip it over and sear the other side, leaving plenty of juicy bites along with the crispy edges.

CHORIZO AND HASH BROWN OVEN OMELET

<table>
<tr><td>Yield:
6 servings</td><td>Those who appreciate the ease of quiche and other egg casseroles will find that the oven omelet simplifies things even further. Without any layers, the ingredients are stirred together and then poured into a baking dish. I love the adaptability of this meal; you can make it with your favorite meats or without any meat at all. I like to serve this with Southwest Garden Salad (page 52) for a great light supper.</td></tr>
</table>

8–9 oz (225–252 g) pork chorizo

8 eggs

½ cup (120 ml) milk

10 oz (280 g) refrigerated hash browns, about 2½ cups

1 cup (120 g) shredded cheese (cheddar and pepper Jack work well)

1¼ tsp (7 g) Crazy Salt Seasoning Mix (page 159)

Green onions, sliced, for serving (optional)

Preheat the oven to 350°F (180°C, or gas mark 4). Lightly grease a 9-inch (23-cm) square pan or a 2½-quart (2.3-L) baking dish. Crumble the chorizo into a large skillet over medium-high heat and cook for 5 minutes. Allow the meat to cool slightly; meanwhile, whisk together the eggs and milk in a large mixing bowl. Add the hash browns, cheese and salt mix to the eggs. Stir to combine and then add the meat to the egg mixture.

Pour the mixture into the greased pan and place in the oven. Bake for 30 minutes, until puffy and lightly browned. Remove from the oven and let cool for 10 minutes. Top with the green onions before serving, if desired.

Cook's Notes: Freshly grated potato or frozen hash browns can be substituted for the refrigerated hash browns listed in the recipe. If using frozen hash browns, allow an additional 3 to 5 minutes for the cooking time.

Cooked and crumbled bacon or sausage can be substituted for the chorizo in this recipe. Alternatively, the meat can be skipped entirely, if that's more to your tastes. Feel free to add (1 cup [70 g] total) leftover roasted broccoli (chopped small), fresh spinach or lightly sautéed onions and bell peppers.

If you do not have Crazy Salt Seasoning Mix in the pantry, you can substitute ½ teaspoon kosher salt, ¼ teaspoon freshly ground black pepper, ¼ teaspoon garlic powder and ¼ teaspoon onion powder.

GREEK CHICKEN

Yield:
6–8 servings

Fresh lemon, a splash of red wine vinegar, dried herbs, garlic and red onion make this simple marinated chicken incredibly flavorful. I like to double this recipe, grill the chicken and serve it with a big batch of Roasted Garlic Smashed Potatoes (page 151) for a dinner with friends. This chicken also works well with the Vegetable Lover's Greek Pasta Salad (page 73) or with Italian Rice Pilaf (page 143).

NOTE: The prep time is 10 minutes, plus 6 to 24 hours' marinating time.

10 small bone-in chicken thighs with skin, about 3 lb (1365 g)

½ small red onion, sliced as thin as possible

6 cloves garlic, thinly sliced

1 cup (240 ml) olive oil

½ cup (120 ml) fresh lemon juice, about 3 large lemons

¼ cup (60 ml) red wine vinegar

1 tbsp (3 g) dried oregano

1½ tsp (1.5 g) dried thyme

2 tsp (12 g) kosher salt

1 tsp (3.5 g) freshly ground black pepper

2 tbsp (6 g) chopped fresh parsley, for serving (optional)

1 lemon, sliced into wedges, for serving (optional)

Place the chicken, onion, garlic, oil, lemon juice, vinegar, oregano, thyme, salt and pepper in a large zip-top freezer bag or an airtight container. Seal tightly and turn several times to distribute and coat all the pieces. Refrigerate the chicken while it marinates for 6 to 8 hours and up to 24 hours.

OVEN DIRECTIONS: Preheat the oven to 400°F (200°C, or gas mark 6) and place an oven rack in the center of the oven. Line a heavy baking sheet with foil and place a wire rack over the foil-lined sheet. Place the marinated chicken skin side up on the wire rack. Discard the marinade with the onions. Roast the chicken for 50 to 60 minutes, until golden brown. Let rest for 5 to 10 minutes after removing from the oven. Sprinkle with the parsley and serve with a wedge of lemon, if desired.

GRILLING INSTRUCTIONS: Preheat the grill for indirect heat; the temperature should be around 300°F (150°C). Place the chicken skin side up on the grill and close the lid. Cook for 30 minutes. Flip the chicken over and close the lid. Cook an additional 20 minutes. Let rest for 5 to 10 minutes after removing from the grill. Sprinkle with the parsley and serve with a wedge of lemon, if desired.

Cook's Notes: For extra-crispy oven-roasted chicken, start with the chicken skin side down, then turn over after 30 minutes in the oven.

The recipe is written for bone-in chicken, but this marinade works just as well on boneless skinless breasts and thighs. Simply monitor the chicken as it cooks and reduce the cooking times, as necessary.

HEARTY ALL-DAY CHILI

Yield:
8–10 servings

Four different beans, beef, green chiles and plenty of spices create a thick and hearty chili that is one of our favorite dinners for the busiest of days. The beef finishes so tender that you can cut it with a spoon, and the beans soften while the chili thickens. Served with as many or as few toppings as we have on hand, this chili makes frequent appearances on our table all winter long.

This is my meal for the days when I know I'm going to be busy with other things all day and yet I still need a dinner plan. I keep these canned ingredients on hand all the time and I can pull almost the entire meal together straight out of the pantry. Best of all, it takes barely ten minutes to combine everything first thing in the morning and it will simmer on its own all day.

1 tbsp (15 ml) olive oil

1½ lb (680 g) beef chuck roast or top round, trimmed and cut into ½-inch (1.3-cm) pieces

1 (15.5-oz [434-g]) can Great Northern or white kidney beans

1 (15.5-oz [434-g]) can light red kidney beans

1 (15.5-oz [434-g]) can black beans

2 (15.5-oz [434-g]) cans pinto beans

1 (15-oz [420-g]) can tomato sauce

1 (14.5-oz [406-g]) can diced tomatoes with juices

1 (4-oz [112-g]) can chopped green chiles

¼ cup (24 g) Mexican Seasoning Mix (page 158) or taco seasoning mix

TOPPING OPTIONS
Sour cream
Cheddar cheese, shredded
Green onions, sliced thin
Yellow onions, chopped small
Fresh tomatoes, chopped
Avocados, chopped
Cilantro, chopped
Corn chips

HEARTY ALL-DAY CHILI (CONT.)

SLOW COOKER DIRECTIONS: Heat a large skillet over medium-high heat. Add the oil to the skillet and when it is shimmering, add the beef. Spread it across the pan and allow it to sear for 2 minutes without stirring. Stir and sear for 2 more minutes. Transfer the beef to the slow cooker.

While the beef is on the stove, combine the Great Northern beans, kidney beans, black beans, pinto beans, tomato sauce, diced tomatoes, green chiles and Mexican Seasoning Mix in the slow cooker. Add the seared meat and stir to combine. Cover with a lid and cook on LOW for 8 to 12 hours. Scoop into bowls and add the toppings of your choice.

STOVE TOP DIRECTIONS: Heat a very large pot over medium-high heat. Add the oil to the pot and when it is shimmering, add the beef. Spread the meat across the bottom of the pot and allow it to sear for 2 minutes without stirring. Stir or flip the pieces over and sear the other sides.

Add the Great Northern beans, kidney beans, black beans, pinto beans, tomato sauce, diced tomatoes, green chiles and Mexican Seasoning Mix and stir to combine. Bring to a simmer, stirring occasionally, and then reduce the heat to low. Keep the chili just barely under a simmer all day or for at least 4 to 6 hours. Stir every 1 to 2 hours until ready to eat. Scoop into bowls and add the toppings of your choice.

*See photo on page 106 (lower right).

Cook's Notes: This chili also works well with a pound (455 g) of cooked and crumbled ground beef, bacon or sausage. Just add the cooked meat to the slow cooker along with the rest of the ingredients. For an extra-hearty chili, we like to cook and crumble a pound (455 g) of hot pork sausage and add it to the chili along with the chuck roast.

It isn't necessary to drain any of the canned items—simply open and pour. Quick tip: When opening canned beans, shake first. This will loosen any beans that might otherwise stick to the sides of the can. Feel free to mix and match your favorite varieties of beans for this chili.

PERFECT BAKED, STUFFED POTATOES

<table>
<tr><td>Yield:
4–6 servings</td><td>Fluffy baked potatoes with a perfectly crispy skin are filled with meats or vegetables and then topped with cheese. While visiting my sister a few years ago, she made BBQ Chicken Stuffed Potatoes, and they've made regular appearances on our table ever since. Perfectly simple, filling and hugely adaptable to each person's tastes, stuffed potatoes are a hit every time I serve them.</td></tr>
</table>

4–6 large russet potatoes

4–6 tsp (20–30 ml) olive oil

½–1 tsp (3–6 g) kosher salt

TOPPING OPTIONS

Shredded cheese

Sour cream

Salsa or hot sauce

Barbecue sauce

Ranch dressing, homemade (page 162) or store-bought

Green onions or chives, thinly sliced

Preheat the oven to 350°F (180°C, or gas mark 4). Scrub the potatoes to remove all dirt and then rinse and dry thoroughly. Poke several holes into each potato with a fork and then place them on a baking sheet. Drizzle each potato with about 1 teaspoon (5 ml) oil and rub lightly with your hands to coat. Generously sprinkle each potato with salt and then place in the oven. Bake for 65 to 75 minutes, until fork tender. When the potatoes are almost finished baking, warm the filling ingredients of your choice (see below). Remove the potatoes from the oven and slice each one down the center and fluff with a fork. Top each potato with the filling. Garnish with the toppings of your choice. Alternatively, you can chop the baked potatoes into bite-size pieces and serve them piled onto a plate and topped with the fillings.

Suggested Combinations

BBQ Chicken Stuffed Potatoes: 3 cups (360 g) chopped chicken + 2 cups (480 ml) barbecue sauce

Vegetable Lover's Potatoes: roasted or steamed vegetables + shredded cheese

Pulled Pork Stuffed Potatoes: Slow Cooker Mexican Pulled Pork (page 122) + 1 cup (240 ml) barbecue sauce

Philly Cheesesteak Potatoes: Philly Cheesesteak Potato Skillet (page 70), minus the potatoes in the recipe

Mexican Beef and Black Bean Potatoes: 1 pound (455 g) cooked ground beef + 1 (14-oz [392-g]) can black beans (drained and rinsed) + 3 tablespoons (18 g) Mexican Seasoning Mix (page 158)

Ham and Cheese with Broccoli: 2 cups (140 g) chopped cooked broccoli + 1 cup (140 g) diced ham + 1 cup (120 g) shredded cheddar, melted together on the potatoes for 5 minutes in the oven

Simple Side Dishes

How can I pick a favorite side dish? Every single one of these side dishes is tasty enough that I've been known to make it and eat it as a meal. Skillet Mexican Street Corn (page 136) is tasty on its own, tossed over Southwest Garden Salad (page 52) or stuffed into burritos with Slow Cooker Mexican Pulled Pork (page 122) and black beans.

Maple Herb Roasted Carrots (page 135) is the recipe that transformed all of my boys into carrot lovers. Sweet Chili Roasted Broccoli (page 144) is my all-time favorite way to serve broccoli. I often roast a tray of this broccoli just for my lunch. It really is that good.

Cajun Roasted Potatoes (page 139) are a terrific side for almost any meal, but we especially love them in our Huevos Rancheros Bowls (page 20). Roasted Garlic Smashed Potatoes (page 151) are the perfect side for Chicken Parmesan Meatloaf (page 118)—without any extra work or oven time, the garlic roasts while the meatloaf cooks.

The Mixed Green Salad with Oranges and Cranberries (page 152) is a popular side dish, but it's also one of my favorite lunches with an extra handful of nuts or grilled chicken on top.

MAPLE HERB ROASTED CARROTS

Yield:
6 servings

Fresh carrots are naturally quite sweet, but roasting them with a maple and herb glaze takes them to a whole new level. While my kids are usually willing to snack on a few raw carrots, these roasted carrots disappear as fast as I can serve them. I like to serve these with Maple Dijon Glazed Pork Tenderloin (page 102) or Crispy Garlic Paprika Chicken (page 114).

2 lb (910 g) full-size carrots, orange or rainbow colored

2 tbsp (30 ml) light-flavored olive oil

2 tbsp (30 ml) maple syrup

1 tbsp (15 ml) honey

2 tbsp (6 g) fresh rosemary, about 1 tbsp chopped

1 tsp (6 g) kosher salt

¼ tsp freshly ground black pepper

2 tbsp (6 g) thinly sliced chives or green onions, for topping (optional)

Preheat the oven to 450°F (230°C, or gas mark 8). Wash and thoroughly dry the carrots. Slice the carrots into 3- to 4-inch (7.5- to 10-cm) lengths and then quarter lengthwise. Place the carrots on a large baking sheet. Whisk together the oil, syrup, honey, rosemary, salt and pepper in a small bowl. Pour over the carrots and toss with your hands to coat thoroughly.

Spread the carrots on the baking sheet and roast in the center of the oven for 15 minutes. Serve at this point for tender and slightly crisp carrots, or stir and roast an additional 10 minutes until the carrots are soft and lightly caramelized. Top with the chives or green onions, if desired.

Cook's Notes: I've made this recipe with both full-size and baby carrots. Both will work, but my preference is for sliced full-size carrots, as they always have more flavor. Baby carrots contain more water and will not caramelize the way the sliced full-size carrots do.

It isn't necessary to peel the carrots for this recipe; however, you may peel them if that is your preference.

SKILLET MEXICAN STREET CORN

Yield:
6 servings

Fresh sweet corn is sautéed with spices before being tossed with lime juice and topped with cilantro, onions and Mexican cheese—all the irresistible flavors of Mexican street corn are combined in this easy skillet recipe. This corn works well as a side dish with Crispy Garlic Paprika Chicken (page 114) or Slow Cooker Mexican Pulled Pork (page 122). The corn is also a terrific addition to tossed salads, burritos or tacos.

5 cups (650 g) fresh corn, from about 6 ears

1 tbsp (14 g) unsalted butter

1 tbsp (14 g) mayonnaise

½ tsp kosher salt

½ tsp chile powder

⅛ tsp cayenne pepper

Juice of 1 lime, about 2 tbsp (30 ml)

2 tbsp (20 g) finely chopped red onion

¼ cup (60 g) crumbled Cotija cheese

¼ cup (12 g) finely chopped cilantro

Lime wedges, for serving (optional)

Remove the kernels from the corn and set aside. Melt the butter in a large nonstick skillet over medium-high heat. Add the corn, mayonnaise, salt, chile powder and cayenne. Stir to coat and cook for about 3 minutes, until hot.

Remove from the heat or transfer to a serving dish. Drizzle with the lime juice and sprinkle with the onion, cheese and cilantro. Stir to combine. Serve with lime wedges, for an extra kick of lime, if desired.

Cook's Notes: This recipe can also be made with (thawed) frozen corn. Drain any excess water off the corn and then follow the recipe as written.

Cotija can usually be found with the dairy products in most grocery stores. Feta cheese can be substituted for the Cotija if necessary.

CAJUN ROASTED POTATOES

Yield:
8–10 servings

Spicy Cajun potatoes are a great side dish for grilled and roasted meats. They are also delicious chopped up with a soft egg on top or tossed into egg burritos with a bit of sausage or bacon. Any leftover potatoes will keep nicely in the refrigerator for a few days and can be reheated in a hot skillet or in the microwave.

5 tbsp (75 ml) olive oil, divided

1 tbsp (7 g) smoked or plain paprika

1 tbsp (3 g) granulated garlic or garlic powder

2 tsp (12 g) kosher salt

2 tsp (5 g) freshly ground black pepper

2 tsp (2 g) granulated onion or onion powder

2 tsp (2 g) dried oregano

2 tsp (2 g) dried thyme

½–1 tsp (1–2 g) cayenne pepper

4 lb (1820 g) small red or yellow potatoes

Unsalted butter, for serving (optional)

Preheat the oven to 450°F (230°C, or gas mark 8). Lightly grease a large baking sheet with 1 tablespoon (15 ml) of the olive oil. Stir together the herbs and spices with the remaining 4 tablespoons (60 ml) oil in a large mixing bowl. Wash and dry the potatoes. Slice each potato in half. Add them to the bowl with the spice mixture and toss well with your hands to thoroughly coat.

Spread the potatoes on the baking pan. Roast for 30 minutes, until the potatoes are tender and beginning to crisp. Stir with a metal spatula and roast for an additional 10 minutes, until lightly browned and crisp. Serve with soft butter on the side, for dipping, if desired.

Cook's Notes: If your potatoes are bigger than 1 to 1½ inches (2.5 to 3.8 cm), you'll want to quarter them (instead of simply halving them) to make sure they pick up plenty of flavor from the seasonings. Adjust the amount of cayenne for less heat, if that is your preference.

BUTTERY GARLIC GREEN BEANS

Yield: 6 servings	These crisp, hot, buttery green beans are coated with garlic and are completely irresistible. The key to making this a quick side dish is blanching the green beans before sautéing them. They will cook in a fraction of the usual sauté time. Serve these beans with Honey Soy Broiled Salmon (page 59), Chicken Parmesan Meatloaf (page 118) or Greek Chicken (page 126).

1 tbsp (18 g) kosher salt (for the cooking water) plus ¼ tsp, to taste, divided

1 lb (455 g) fresh French green beans or haricot vert

1 tbsp (14 g) unsalted butter

1 tbsp (15 ml) light-flavored olive oil

4 cloves garlic, minced

¼ tsp freshly ground black pepper

Bring a large pot of water to a boil over high heat. Add 1 tablespoon (18 g) of the salt to the pot and then add the green beans. Cover with a lid, set a timer for 2 minutes and bring to a boil again. While the beans are on the stove, fill a large mixing bowl with ice water. Set the bowl of ice water next to the sink and place a strainer in the sink.

When the timer beeps, check the beans; they should be almost tender, but still crisp. Pour the beans from the boiling water into the strainer and then transfer them to the ice water. When the beans are cold, pour them back through the strainer and then lightly pat them dry with a tea towel.

Heat a large skillet over medium heat and add the butter and oil. When the butter melts, add the garlic and stir. Let it cook for 30 seconds, until the buttery garlic is frothy and fragrant. Add the beans and stir to coat. Sprinkle with the remaining ¼ teaspoon salt and the pepper. Toss with tongs and continue tossing and stirring for 3 to 4 minutes, until the beans are hot and well coated with buttery garlic. Taste the green beans and adjust the salt, if desired.

Cook's Notes: If you're unfamiliar with blanching vegetables, don't let that part of this recipe intimidate you. After you've done this a couple of times, you'll be surprised at how quickly this dish can be prepared. It's as simple as boiling, dunking in ice water and sautéing.

If you're using bigger green beans, add an extra 1 to 2 minutes to the boiling time. Just check for doneness and plunge them into the ice water as soon as they are cooked to your liking.

ITALIAN RICE PILAF

Yield:
6 servings

Buttery rice pilaf with fresh herbs is a great side dish for almost any meal. I serve this rice with Greek Chicken (page 126) and Maple Dijon Glazed Pork Tenderloin (page 102).

2 tbsp (28 g) unsalted butter

1 cup (100 g) short ½-inch (1.3-cm) vermicelli or orzo pasta

1 cup (165 g) jasmine rice or plain long-grain white rice

4 cups (960 ml) water

2 tbsp (30 g) chicken base or bouillon

⅛–¼ tsp crushed red pepper flakes

6 large fresh basil leaves, very thinly sliced*

2 tsp (2 g) fresh rosemary, minced*

2 tsp (2 g) fresh oregano*

2 tsp (2 g) fresh thyme*

1 tbsp (3 g) chopped fresh Italian parsley

¼–½ tsp kosher salt, if needed

Melt the butter in a large skillet over medium-high heat. Add the pasta and stir to coat. Sauté for 3 to 5 minutes, stirring frequently, until the pasta is lightly browned. Add the rice, water, chicken base and red pepper flakes. Bring to a boil, stir and reduce the heat to low, making sure it is still simmering, and cover with a lid.

Cook for 16 minutes and check to see if the rice is tender and the water has been absorbed. Add the fresh herbs, stir and taste. Cook for an additional 1 to 2 minutes if the water has not been absorbed. Remove from the heat. Taste and add salt if needed. Let rest for 5 minutes and fluff with a fork before serving.

Cook's Note: While fresh herbs are always my first choice, dried Italian herbs can be substituted for the fresh herbs marked with an *. Use a total of 1 tablespoon (7 g) Italian seasoning, homemade (page 159) or store-bought, to replace the fresh herbs. If you are using dried herbs for the ingredients marked with an *, add them along with the water to cook with the rice. Be sure to taste the pilaf and adjust the salt of the recipe at the end, because different brands of chicken base and bouillon will vary in saltiness.

SWEET CHILI ROASTED BROCCOLI

Yield: 4 servings	Crisp, sweet and slightly spicy broccoli is a great side dish for almost any meal. Served over rice, this broccoli becomes a deliciously casual lunch.

6 cups (420 g) broccoli florets, approximately 2 medium-size heads broccoli

2 tbsp (30 ml) light-flavored olive oil

2 tbsp (30 ml) honey

2 tsp (10 g) Sambal Oelek chili paste

1 tsp (6 g) kosher salt

Preheat the oven to 450°F (230°C, or gas mark 8). Wash the broccoli and then shake it dry or wrap it in a tea towel and blot well to remove as much water as possible. Place the broccoli on a large baking sheet. Whisk together the oil, honey, chili paste and salt in a small bowl. Drizzle over the broccoli and toss with your hands to coat thoroughly.

Roast the broccoli in the center of the oven for 10 minutes. Stir and roast an additional 2 to 3 minutes, until slightly crisp and browned on the edges.

PARMESAN HERB POTATOES

Yield:
6–8 servings

Red potatoes are coated lightly with oil, sprinkled with herbs and spices and roasted until golden brown. The warm potatoes are tossed with Parmesan and roasted once more until the cheese has melted and the potatoes are slightly crisp. Serve these potatoes with an egg on top for a simple meal or as a side for Greek Chicken (page 126) or Maple Dijon Glazed Pork Tenderloin (page 102). These potatoes disappear almost before they have a chance to cool.

2½ lb (1138 g) small red potatoes, chopped into ½-inch (1.3-cm) pieces

2 tbsp (30 ml) olive oil

1 tbsp (3 g) minced fresh rosemary or 2 tsp (2 g) Italian seasoning, homemade (page 159) or store-bought

1 tsp (6 g) kosher salt

½ tsp freshly ground black pepper

½ tsp granulated garlic

1 cup (100 g) freshly grated Parmesan or Pecorino Romano, divided

Preheat the oven to 425°F (220°C, or gas mark 7). Place the potatoes on a baking sheet, drizzle with the oil and sprinkle with all the herbs and spices. Toss with your hands to thoroughly coat and then spread on the pan.

Roast for 20 minutes on the middle oven rack. Remove from the oven and stir with a spatula. Sprinkle with ½ cup (50 g) of the cheese and stir again. Spread the potatoes on the baking pan again and sprinkle with the remaining ½ cup (50 g) cheese. Roast for 5 more minutes, until the cheese has melted and the potatoes are slightly browned.

Cook's Note: This recipe can be doubled. You'll want to allow an additional 5 to 6 minutes of cooking time and use two baking sheets, in order to spread the potatoes out enough to allow browning.

TANGY CABBAGE SLAW

Yield:
6–8 servings

This sweet and tangy crunchy cabbage slaw is my favorite kind of coleslaw. I like to serve this slaw alongside Crunchy Honey Lime Chicken (page 28) or layered onto pulled pork sandwiches (pork recipe on page 122).

3 cups (210 g) finely shredded green cabbage

1 cup (70 g) finely shredded purple cabbage

¼ cup (60 ml) apple cider vinegar

2 tbsp (25 g) sugar

1–2 tbsp (15–30 ml) fresh lime juice, to taste

1 tbsp (15 ml) light-flavored olive oil

½ tsp freshly ground black pepper

½ tsp celery seed

¼ tsp kosher salt

Place the shredded cabbage in a medium-size mixing bowl. Stir together the vinegar, sugar, 1 tablespoon (15 ml) of the lime juice, oil, pepper, celery seed and salt. Pour the dressing over the cabbage. Toss well to coat. Taste the slaw and adjust the lime juice, salt and pepper, if needed. Serve immediately or refrigerate until ready to eat.

Cook's Note: A 14-ounce (392-g) bag of shredded coleslaw mix, either classic or tricolor, can be substituted for the green and purple cabbages in this recipe.

ROASTED GARLIC SMASHED POTATOES

Yield:
8 servings

Roasted garlic is something like a secret weapon for creating dishes that taste a whole lot fancier than they really are. The time involved in these mashed potatoes might look like a lot (with the hour for roasting the garlic) but the actual work involved takes less than 10 minutes total. There is no need to peel the potatoes in this recipe.

Serve the potatoes with Chicken Parmesan Meatloaf (page 118), All-Day Beef Brisket (page 117) or Green Chile and Cheese Stuffed Chicken (page 68). Toss the garlic in the oven to roast while the oven is preheating and then continue roasting the garlic along with the main dish. Right before making the potatoes, pull the garlic out.

SHORTCUT TIP: You can substitute 1 teaspoon (1 g) of granulated garlic or garlic powder for the roasted garlic in this recipe. The flavor won't be quite the same, but the potatoes will still be tasty.

2 heads garlic

2 tsp (10 ml) olive oil

3 lb (1365 g) Yukon gold potatoes, chopped into 1-inch (2.5-cm) pieces

2 tbsp (36 g) plus 1 tsp (6 g) kosher salt, divided

4 tbsp (56 g) unsalted butter, at room temperature

¼ cup (60 ml) milk, plus more to taste

½ tsp freshly ground black pepper

Cook's Note: If you won't be using it right away, extra roasted garlic can be stored in the refrigerator for several days. Store the garlic in an airtight container, unless you'd like everything else in the refrigerator to have a rich garlic aroma as well!

To roast the garlic, preheat the oven to 400°F (200°C, or gas mark 6). Slice the top (the non-root end) off the heads of garlic. Place each head of garlic on a small piece of foil and drizzle a teaspoon (5 ml) of olive oil over the top of each. Wrap loosely in the foil. Place the wrapped garlic on a baking tray.

Roast for approximately 50 minutes, until the garlic gives slightly when squeezed with a pair of tongs. The head of garlic should be soft and golden brown.

Carefully remove from the oven and let cool. Unwrap and use your fingers to squeeze the roasted garlic out of the paper skins. Smash the roasted garlic with a fork, and set aside 1 to 2 tablespoons (10 to 20 g).

While the garlic is roasting, place the chopped potatoes in a large pot, cover with water and add 2 tablespoons (36 g) of the salt. Cover with a lid and bring to a boil, uncover and boil until the potatoes are fork tender but not falling apart, about 20 minutes. Drain the potatoes and then transfer them back to the empty pot.

Place the pot with the potatoes back over the warm (but turned off) burner; if you have a gas stove, turn the heat to the lowest possible setting. (This will help evaporate any water left in the pan and keep the mashed potatoes nice and fluffy.) Smash the potatoes with a potato masher and then add the butter, milk, remaining 1 teaspoon (6 g) salt, pepper and 1 tablespoon (10 g) of the roasted garlic. Stir to combine; taste the potatoes and add more milk, salt, pepper or garlic as desired.

MIXED GREEN SALAD WITH ORANGES AND CRANBERRIES

Yield:
4–6 servings

Sweet oranges and cranberries are mixed with crunchy caramelized almonds and slivered red onion in this baby spinach and arugula salad. The simple drizzle of juice from the oranges is truly all the dressing this salad needs, but it can be made even better with a drizzle of White Balsamic Vinaigrette. This salad pairs well with Greek Chicken (page 126), Sweet and Spicy Salmon with Broccoli (page 27) or Chicken Cordon Bleu Sliders (page 19).

8 oz (225 g) baby spinach leaves, roughly chopped

4 oz (115 g) arugula (optional)

1 small red onion, very thinly sliced

1 (11-oz [308-g]) can mandarin oranges, drained, 2 tbsp (30 ml) liquid reserved

⅔ cup (80 g) dried sweetened cranberries

½ cup (75 g) caramelized almonds, homemade (recipe below) or store-bought

¼ cup (60 ml) White Balsamic Vinaigrette (page 161, optional)

¼–½ cup (38–75 g) crumbled feta cheese

Combine the spinach, arugula, if desired, onion, oranges, cranberries and almonds in a large mixing bowl. Toss to combine and drizzle with the reserved liquid from the oranges. Drizzle with the vinaigrette, if desired. Sprinkle the feta across the salad.

Cook's Note: Feel free to skip the arugula. I've also made this salad with spring mix, and with or without a separate dressing. Most of the time, I tend to make this particular salad exactly as written. If you want to dress it up a bit more though, White Balsamic Vinaigrette (page 161) is my recommendation.

Yield:
½ cup (75 g)

CARAMELIZED ALMONDS

1 tsp (5 g) unsalted butter

½ cup (75 g) sliced almonds

1 tbsp (12 g) sugar

In a large skillet, melt the butter over medium-high heat. When it is just starting to foam, add the almonds and stir to coat them with butter. When the almonds are hot and slightly toasty, sprinkle with the sugar and stir constantly as it melts onto them. This should only take a few minutes.

After the sugar has caramelized and the nuts have turned slightly brown, remove from the heat and immediately pour the almonds onto a piece of parchment paper or a silicone mat. Using two forks, separate them to prevent them from clumping as they cool. Once cool, serve or store in an airtight container.

SIMPLE ROASTED VEGETABLES

Yield:
3–4 servings

Roasted vegetables are on our dinner table multiple nights a week. Just a drizzle of oil and a sprinkling of salt and pepper are all it takes to bring out the natural sweetness and deepen the flavors of the vegetables.

I keep most of these vegetables in the refrigerator year-round for quick and easy side dishes. Mix and match the different vegetables however you like best. The ratios below are per pound (455 g) of vegetables. I typically roast 1 to 2 pounds (455 to 910 g) of vegetables at a time.

1 lb (455 g) fresh vegetables

1 tbsp (15 ml) olive oil

½ tsp kosher salt

¼ tsp freshly ground black pepper

Preheat the oven to 450°F (230°C, or gas mark 8). Wash, trim and cut the vegetables into bite-size pieces. Place the vegetables on a half-size baking sheet pan. Drizzle with the olive oil and sprinkle with the salt and pepper. Spread on the tray and roast in the center of the oven for approximately 10 minutes, until slightly tender and lightly browned on the edges.

Approximate Cooking Times for 1 Pound (455 g) of Vegetables

Asparagus, ends trimmed: 10–12 minutes

Broccoli, cut into bite-size florets: 10–12 minutes

Brussels sprouts, medium size, halved: 10–12 minutes

Carrots, whole or cut bite-size: 13–15 minutes

Cauliflower, cut into bite-size florets: 15–18 minutes

French green beans: 10–12 minutes

Large green beans, cut bite-size: 12–13 minutes

Sweet yellow onions, cut into wedges: 10–12 minutes

Zucchini, cut bite-size: 8–10 minutes

Condiments and Spices

Using a premixed blend of spices doesn't take any more time than the usual sprinkling of salt and pepper and yet it adds so much flavor to any dish! Feel free to multiply the seasoning mixes however you like. I typically double or triple these recipes and keep large batches of them ready to use in my spice cabinet.

As with making my own spice blends, salad dressings take only a few minutes to stir or shake together. There is nothing I've found in a store that can compare with a simple dressing made fresh at home, and once you taste the flavor of fresh dressings you will find it hard to go back to the store-bought options.

White Balsamic (page 161), Bold Italian (page 160), Ranch (page 162), Honey Mustard (page 161) and the Chipotle Lime Vinaigrette from the Southwest Garden Salad (page 52) are the dressings I make more than any others. I've been making this ranch dressing for years now, and it's an unusual day when the kids aren't pulling it out of the refrigerator along with a box of raw vegetables to snack on mid-afternoon.

MEXICAN SEASONING MIX

Yield:
About 1 cup
(150 g)

This blend of Mexican herbs and spices has lived in my kitchen for years now. The seasoning mix can be used in any recipe that calls for taco seasoning. The beauty of this recipe is the ability to adjust the heat however you like it best. If you find it a bit spicy, reduce the chile powder and pepper. Want a little more kick? Increase them.

½ cup (56 g) chile powder

4 tbsp (28 g) ground cumin

2 tbsp (36 g) kosher salt

2 tbsp (12 g) freshly ground black pepper

4 tsp (9 g) smoked paprika

2 tsp (2 g) crushed red pepper flakes

2 tsp (2 g) dried oregano

2 tsp (2 g) granulated garlic or garlic powder

2 tsp (2 g) granulated onion or onion powder

1 tsp (2 g) cayenne pepper (optional)

Combine all the spices in a jar and stir or shake to combine. Store in the pantry until needed.

*See photo on page 156.

Cook's Note: If you have access to it, New Mexico chile powder is my choice for this spice mixture and for any other recipe that calls for chile powder. You should be able to find it in spice pouches in the Mexican food section of most grocery stores.

ITALIAN SEASONING MIX

Yield: About ¼ cup (18 g)	This Italian Seasoning Mix combines classic Italian flavors in an easy-to-use dried blend of herbs. Not only is this my favorite soup seasoning, but I also use this blend of herbs for pasta sauces, potatoes and roasted meats.

1 tbsp (3 g) dried basil

1 tbsp (3 g) dried oregano

1 tbsp (3 g) dried thyme

1 tbsp (3 g) dried marjoram

2 tsp (2 g) dried sage

1 tbsp (3 g) dried rosemary

Combine the basil, oregano, thyme, marjoram and sage in a small jar. Lightly crush the large pieces of rosemary with your fingers before adding it to the jar. Stir or seal with a lid and shake to combine.

*See photo on page 156.

CRAZY SALT SEASONING MIX

Yield: About ½ cup (84 g)	I use Crazy Salt Seasoning Mix on eggs, meat, popcorn, vegetables, French fries and any kind of potato. You can use this spice blend anywhere you might want a sprinkling of salt, but it is especially amazing on eggs. Eggs just aren't eggs in my house without the Crazy Salt.

¼ cup (72 g) kosher salt

4 tsp (4 g) granulated garlic

1 tbsp (6 g) freshly ground black pepper

2 tsp (2 g) granulated onion

½ tsp celery salt

½ tsp cayenne pepper

¼ tsp finely crushed sage (optional)

Combine all the spices in a jar and stir or shake to combine. Store in an airtight container until ready to use.

*See photo on page 156.

Cook's Note: You can pulse all the spices in a blender for a finer, more uniform consistency or simply stir them together in a jar. I tend to measure Crazy Salt Seasoning Mix in finger pinches, the same way I use kosher salt, so the jar method works great for me. Just shake the jar if the spices begin to separate.

CAJUN SEASONING MIX

Yield:
About ¼ cup
(35 g)

These are the spices I use when making the Cajun-Rubbed Chicken or Pork Chops (page 121). I love this combination of spices so much that I keep a batch in the pantry and use it frequently. Sprinkled on Simple Roasted Vegetables (page 155) or potatoes, it has a fantastic flavor.

1 tbsp (7 g) smoked or plain paprika

1 tbsp (3 g) granulated garlic or garlic powder

2 tsp (12 g) kosher salt

2 tsp (5 g) freshly ground black pepper

2 tsp (2 g) granulated onion or onion powder

2 tsp (2 g) crushed oregano

2 tsp (2 g) crushed thyme

1 tsp (2 g) cayenne pepper

Stir the herbs and spices together in a small jar or seal with a lid and shake to combine.

*See photo on page 156.

BOLD ITALIAN SALAD DRESSING

Yield:
About 1¼ cups
(300 ml)

The ever-popular oil and vinegar salad dressing is kicked up with a sprinkling of red pepper flakes and an extra splash of citrus for plenty of tang in this bold Italian dressing.

½ cup (120 ml) olive oil

⅓ cup (80 ml) lemon juice

⅓ cup (80 ml) red wine vinegar

3 cloves garlic, minced

2 tbsp (6 g) fresh oregano or 2 tsp (2 g) dried

1 tsp (6 g) kosher salt

½–¾ tsp crushed red pepper flakes

½ tsp freshly ground black pepper

Combine all the ingredients in a glass jar and whisk or shake well. Cover tightly with a lid and refrigerate until needed.

*See photo on page 163.

WHITE BALSAMIC VINAIGRETTE

Yield:
About ¾ cup
(177 ml)

This sweet balsamic vinaigrette has been one of my personal favorites for a few years now. I especially love it on any salad that combines greens and fruit.

½ cup (120 ml) light-flavored olive oil

¼ cup (60 ml) white balsamic or champagne vinegar

3 tbsp (36 g) white sugar

1 tsp (6 g) kosher salt

½ tsp freshly ground black pepper

Combine all the ingredients in a small jar and shake to blend. Store in the refrigerator until ready to serve.

*See photo on page 163.

Cook's Note: This can also be made with traditional balsamic vinegar; the dressing will be a darker color.

HONEY MUSTARD DIPPING SAUCE AND SALAD DRESSING

Yield:
About 1¼ cups
(300 ml)

With plenty of tangy mustard flavor balanced by sweet honey, this is a great dressing for salads or a dipping sauce for chicken.

⅔ cup (160 g) mayonnaise

¼ cup (44 g) Dijon mustard

¼ cup (60 ml) honey

2 tbsp (30 ml) white vinegar

¼ tsp kosher salt

Whisk together all the ingredients in a small bowl. Pour into a glass jar or airtight container. Cover and chill in the refrigerator until needed.

*See photo on page 163.

RANCH DRESSING

Yield:
About 2 cups
(480 g)

Homemade ranch dressing puts to shame anything you can purchase in a store; there's just nothing like it. I make this with dried herbs most of the time, because I always have them on hand. However, any time fresh herbs are at my fingertips, they are my first choice.

⅔ cup (160 g) mayonnaise

⅔ cup (160 g) sour cream

½ cup (120 ml) milk

1 tbsp (10 g) finely minced yellow onion or 1 tsp (1 g) granulated onion or onion powder

1 tbsp (10 g) finely minced garlic or 1 tsp (1 g) granulated garlic or garlic powder

2 tbsp (6 g) finely chopped fresh dill or 2 tsp (2 g) dried

1½ tbsp (4.5 g) finely chopped fresh chives or 1½ tsp (1.5 g) dried

1½ tbsp (4.5 g) finely chopped fresh Italian parsley or 1½ tsp (1.5 g) dried

1 tsp (6 g) kosher salt

½ tsp freshly ground black pepper

1–2 tbsp (15–30 ml) fresh lemon juice or white wine vinegar, to taste

Combine all the ingredients in a small bowl and whisk to blend. Chill for at least 1 to 2 hours prior to serving. Keeps well in the refrigerator for up to a week.

Stress-Free Desserts

Some nights require dessert. Whether you're planning a casual dinner and simply want something sweet to share or you're hosting a fancier meal for guests, it's a wonderful thing to be able to place a mouthwatering dessert on the table. With a maximum of fifteen minutes of hands-on time, all of the recipes in this chapter are guaranteed to be stress free and are certain to impress with a minimum of effort.

From Lemon Lover's Pound Cake (page 167) to Creamy Peanut Butter Mousse (page 172) and Never-Fail Blondies (page 183), this final chapter is full of recipes to make when time is limited and you want a sweet treat. If you have chocolate lovers in your life, the Chocolate-Glazed Chocolate Chip Pound Cake (page 179) is going to be their dream come true. Want something a little lighter for serving with coffee or tea? Try the Raspberry Almond Coffee Cake (page 171).

A few years ago, my son Benjamin developed a sensitivity to gluten. In the time since, I have worked to convert and develop recipes for gluten-free breads and sweets that taste as delicious as their traditional counterparts. I've provided gluten-free substitutions for all of the recipes included in this book. As with anything else, use your own judgment in selecting ingredients. If you are dealing with an allergy, read the labels and know your gluten-free ingredients.

LEMON LOVER'S POUND CAKE

Yield:
12–18 servings

Tart lemon flavor fills this pound cake along with a hint of almond and just enough sweetness to balance it. This is an incredibly moist cake that slices beautifully and is sure to impress. This has become one of my favorite company desserts and it receives rave reviews from everyone who tastes it.

CAKE
¾ cup (168 g) unsalted butter, at room temperature

2½ cups (500 g) sugar

4 large eggs

2 tsp (10 ml) almond extract

⅔ cup (160 ml) fresh lemon juice, about 5 large lemons

¼ cup (24 g) lemon zest, about 4 large lemons

2¼ cups (270 g) all-purpose flour*

1 tsp (3 g) baking powder

½ tsp kosher salt

GLAZE
2 tbsp (28 g) unsalted butter

1½ cups (180 g) powdered sugar

2 tbsp (30 ml) fresh lemon juice

½ tsp almond extract

* GLUTEN-FREE SUBSTITUTION
1½ cups (222 g) brown rice flour

⅔ cup (85 g) tapioca starch

⅓ cup (59 g) potato starch

1½ tsp (7 g) xanthan gum

To make the cake, preheat the oven to 325°F (170°C, or gas mark 3). Arrange an oven rack in the center of the oven. Thoroughly grease and lightly flour an 8- or 10-cup (1900- or 2400-ml) Bundt pan.

In a large bowl, beat the butter and sugar together on medium speed until fluffy crumbs form. Add the eggs and almond extract, and beat again until smooth. Add the lemon juice and zest, and beat on low speed to combine. Add the flour, baking powder and salt. Beat again, just until combined.

Pour the batter into the prepared pan. Bake for 60 to 65 minutes, until golden on top and light brown on the edges. Cool in the pan on a wire rack for 15 minutes. After 15 minutes, place the cooling rack on top of the cake, hold the sides firmly and invert the pan over the rack. The cake should drop smoothly out of the pan. Tap firmly on the pan with a wooden spoon, if necessary, to free the cake from the pan. Let the cake cool completely before glazing.

To make the glaze, melt the butter in a small glass bowl. Add the powdered sugar, lemon juice and almond extract. Whisk together until smooth. The glaze should pour off the spoon in a white stream. Add a teaspoon (5 ml) more juice to thin it or 1 to 2 tablespoons (8 to 16 g) more powdered sugar to thicken it, if necessary. Drizzle the glaze over the cake. Store at room temperature, loosely covered, preferably not airtight. This cake will keep nicely and stay very moist for 3 or 4 days.

CRUNCHY NO-BAKE CHOCOLATE PEANUT BUTTER BARS

Yield:
48 bite-size pieces or 12–16 "candy bar" size pieces

This crunchy chocolate peanut butter treat is the best homemade candy in town. I have been making versions of this "candy bar" ever since I was a little girl at summer camp. This homemade candy trumps anything store-bought by a mile. My favorite part? My youngest son Nate is five years old and he loves to help me make this dessert. It's one of his favorite treats and it takes just a few minutes to stir together, even with his "help."

1½ cups (263 g) semisweet chocolate chips

1 cup (120 ml) creamy peanut butter

½ cup (120 ml) honey

¼ cup (56 g) unsalted butter

3 cups (120 g) regular cornflakes

Place the chocolate chips, peanut butter, honey and butter in a large glass mixing bowl. Microwave for 2 minutes at full power. Remove from the microwave and stir until the chocolate has completely melted and everything is well combined.

Stir in the cornflakes and then pour the candy mixture into an 8-inch (20-cm) square pan. Smooth the mixture across the pan and then refrigerate until firm, at least 2 to 4 hours. Slice with a sharp knife and store in an airtight container in the refrigerator for up to 2 weeks.

Cook's Notes: Feel free to substitute frosted flakes or crisp rice cereal for the cornflakes in this recipe. I've made these bars using all different kinds of crunchy cereals. Coconut oil may also be substituted for the butter in this recipe. Lining the pan with parchment paper will make it easier to remove the bars and slice them.

RASPBERRY ALMOND COFFEE CAKE

Yield:
8–12 servings

Tender cake layered with raspberry sauce and then topped with buttery brown sugar crumbs makes for one heck of a treat, whether you enjoy it with your morning coffee or after dinner. The berry layer stays nice and gooey and the crumb topping is crisp and just buttery enough to melt in your mouth. Don't let yourself be intimidated by the length of the ingredients list. The cake comes together very quickly.

RASPBERRY LAYER

2½ cups (375 g) frozen raspberries

⅓ cup (65 g) sugar

¼ cup (60 ml) water

1 tbsp (15 ml) fresh lemon juice

2 tbsp (16 g) cornstarch

CAKE

½ cup (112 g) unsalted butter, softened, plus more for the pan

1 cup (200 g) sugar

2 eggs

2 tsp (10 ml) almond extract

1 tsp (5 ml) vanilla extract

1 cup (120 g) all-purpose flour*

½ tsp baking powder

½ cup (120 g) sour cream

* GLUTEN-FREE SUBSTITUTION

⅔ cup (98 g) brown rice flour

¼ cup (32 g) tapioca starch

¼ cup (44 g) potato starch

TOPPING

¼ cup (56) unsalted butter

⅔ cup (80 g) all-purpose or brown rice flour (98 g)

⅓ cup (75 g) packed brown sugar

To make the raspberry layer, combine the raspberries, sugar, water, lemon juice and cornstarch in a small saucepan over medium-high heat. Bring to a boil, reduce the heat and simmer for about 5 minutes. Stir and smash the raspberries occasionally. When the berry sauce thickens slightly and coats the back of a spoon, remove from the heat. While the berries are simmering, begin making the rest of the cake.

To make the cake, preheat the oven to 350°F (180°C, or gas mark 4). Grease an 8-inch (20-cm) square pan with butter. In a large bowl, beat the butter and sugar together until light and fluffy, 3 to 4 minutes. Stir in the eggs, almond extract and vanilla extract. Add the flour and baking powder and stir to combine. Mix in the sour cream.

Pour half of the batter into the prepared pan. Spread across the bottom of the pan. Pour the raspberry sauce over the batter and spoon the remaining batter over the raspberry sauce. Smooth lightly with a spatula.

To make the topping, melt the butter in a small bowl in the microwave, add the flour and sugar and stir lightly with a fork to combine. Sprinkle the topping over the cake in the pan.

Bake for 38 to 42 minutes, until lightly browned and a toothpick comes out with moist crumbs and berry juice. Let cool completely before slicing.

Cook's Note: During berry season, fresh raspberries can be substituted for the frozen berries. When they aren't in season, frozen is a great option and both types work well in this recipe.

CREAMY PEANUT BUTTER MOUSSE

Yield:
12–16 servings

Creamy peanut butter mousse is an impressive dessert that takes less than ten minutes to make. This is a seriously rich dessert, perfect for feeding a crowd. I typically serve this sliced from the pan, but I've also served it in small cups with shaved chocolate on top. It's a guaranteed winner of a dessert!

1 cup (240 ml) heavy cream

8 oz (225 g) cream cheese

1 cup (260 g) creamy peanut butter

1 tsp (5 ml) vanilla extract

1 cup (120 g) powdered sugar

2–3 tbsp (30–45 ml) milk

Shaved chocolate, for topping (optional)

Finely chopped peanuts, for topping (optional)

Pour the cream into a mixing bowl and beat with an electric mixer until peaks form, 2 to 3 minutes. Scoop the whipped cream into a small bowl and set in the refrigerator.

Combine the cream cheese, peanut butter and vanilla in the mixing bowl and beat until smooth, about 2 minutes. Add the powdered sugar and beat again for about 1 minute. Add the milk and beat until smooth and creamy, about 30 seconds.

Use a spatula to gently fold and stir in the whipped cream until combined. Transfer to an 8-inch (20-cm) square pan, a medium-size bowl or individual serving dishes. Top with the shaved chocolate and chopped peanuts, if desired. Serve immediately or chill until firm.

Cook's Notes: To shave the chocolate, simply run a vegetable peeler in short strokes along the edge of a bar of chocolate. The result will be lovely curls of chocolate. My preference for this recipe is a very dark chocolate, but any plain chocolate candy bar will work.

When serving this for guests or for potluck-style events, I usually sprinkle a few nuts on top. It's a visual reminder that there are nuts involved, plus I really like the little crunch.

CINNAMON TOAST CAKE

Yield:
9 servings

With a flavor like cinnamon rolls and a topping that is the ultimate cinnamon toast crunch, this cake is an awesome surprise. If you love cinnamon toast, this is the cake for you. The sides of the cake form a phenomenal buttery, cinnamon crunch layer. I've served this cake for breakfast, an afternoon snack or a late-night dessert; it is irresistible at any time of the day.

I made this cake for the first time when I was a little girl. It is one of the first things I remember baking. It is a wonderfully easy recipe that even my kids can now stir together without any trouble at all. This is a cake that has never failed to impress. It might look simple and unimpressive at first glance, but one bite is all it takes to win a person over. With just a few ingredients that are likely to already be in the pantry, this has been one of my favorite desserts for more than twenty years.

CAKE
2 cups (240 g) all-purpose flour*

1 cup (200 g) sugar

2 tsp (6 g) baking powder

1 tsp (6 g) kosher salt

1 cup (240 ml) milk

1 tsp (5 ml) vanilla extract

2 tbsp (28 g) unsalted butter, melted and semi-cooled

TOPPING
½ cup (112 g) unsalted butter, melted

½ cup (100 g) sugar

1 tbsp (8 g) ground cinnamon

* GLUTEN-FREE SUBSTITUTION
1¼ cups (185 g) brown rice flour

½ cup (64 g) tapioca starch

¼ cup (44 g) potato starch

Preheat the oven to 350°F (180°F, or gas mark 4). Grease a 10-inch (25-cm) square pan (an 8- or 9-inch [20- or 23-cm] pan also works).

To make the cake, whisk together the flour, sugar, baking powder and salt in a large bowl. Stir in the milk, vanilla and butter. Pour the batter into the pan and bake for 25 minutes (27 minutes for an 8-inch [20-cm] pan).

To make the topping, while the cake is baking, combine the melted butter, sugar and cinnamon in a bowl and whisk together. Remove the cake from the oven after 25 minutes and pour the topping across the cake. Bake the cake for an additional 10 minutes, until the cinnamon layer is bubbling. Let cool before serving.

Cook's Note: Pour the topping mostly around the sides first and then lightly across the top. I've found that if I pour it all on the center of the cake immediately, it will cause the cake to fall slightly. The cake is still delicious that way, but not as pretty.

LEMON CURD MINI CHEESECAKES

Yield:
15–16 mini cheesecakes

Creamy cheesecake swirled with sweetly tart lemon curd is a hit for any occasion. Picnics, potlucks, special events, birthdays—I would happily take these miniature cheesecakes in lieu of my next birthday cake! These little cheesecakes are firm enough to hold in your hand for a party, but they're also lovely when served on small plates for a special occasion.

CRUST
1¼ cups (100 g) graham cracker crumbs, about 10 crackers

½ cup (112 g) unsalted butter, melted

¼ cup (55 g) packed light brown sugar

FILLING
24 oz (672 g) cream cheese, at room temperature

½ cup (100 g) granulated sugar

¼ cup (55 g) packed light brown sugar

1 tsp (5 ml) vanilla extract

3 eggs

½ cup (120 g) lemon curd

Preheat the oven to 325°F (170°C, or gas mark 3). Prepare a muffin or cupcake tin with 15 or 16 liners.

To make the crust, mix together the graham cracker crumbs, melted butter and brown sugar in a small bowl. Scoop 1 tablespoon (12 g) of the crust mixture into the bottom of each of the prepared liners. Press down the mixture with a small measuring cup or the bottom of a drinking glass.

To make the filling, in a bowl, beat the cream cheese and both sugars together on high speed until smooth. Add the vanilla and the eggs. Beat again on medium speed until the mixture is smooth. Scoop 3 to 4 tablespoons (45 to 60 g) of the filling over the crusts, filling each cup almost to the top. Spoon 1 teaspoon (5 g) of lemon curd on top of each cupcake and swirl lightly with a toothpick.

Bake for 24 minutes and then remove from the oven. The cheesecakes will be puffy and rounded when you remove them from the oven, but they will sink as they cool. Let cool at room temperature for about an hour, then transfer to the refrigerator and chill for at least 4 hours.

Cook's Notes: Gluten-free graham crackers may be substituted if desired. If you want to play with the recipe a bit, swap in caramel sauce, chocolate sauce or other fruit purees for the lemon curd.

CHOCOLATE-GLAZED CHOCOLATE CHIP POUND CAKE

Yield:
12–24 servings

This is a rich pound cake filled with chocolate chips and pecans, frosted with a perfectly smooth chocolate ganache glaze. It is a dream come true for any chocolate lover. This cake slices beautifully whether the slices are generously thick or dainty and thin, making it perfect for a casual dinner or a special occasion.

This recipe is dedicated to my friend Joan. She was taken from us far too early, but her love for chocolate will live on forever.

CAKE
¾ cup (168 g) unsalted butter, at room temperature

1⅔ cups (374 g) packed light brown sugar

¾ cup (150 g) granulated sugar

4 large eggs

1 tbsp (15 ml) vanilla extract

¾ cup (180 ml) milk

2½ cups (300 g) all-purpose flour*

1 tsp (3 g) baking powder

½ tsp kosher salt

2 cups (350 g) semisweet chocolate chips

1 cup (110 g) chopped pecans (optional)

GLAZE
1½ cups (263 g) semisweet chocolate chips

½ cup (112 g) unsalted butter

* GLUTEN-FREE SUBSTITUTION
1½ cups (222 g) brown rice flour

¾ cup (96 g) tapioca starch

½ cup (88 g) potato starch

1½ tsp (7 g) xanthan gum

Preheat the oven to 325°F (170°C, or gas mark 3). Arrange an oven rack in the center of the oven. Thoroughly grease and lightly flour a 12-cup (2880-ml) Bundt pan and set aside.

To make the cake, in a large bowl, beat the butter and sugars together on medium speed until fluffy crumbs form. Add the eggs and vanilla and beat again until smooth. Add the milk and beat on low speed to combine. Add the flour, baking powder and salt. Beat again, just until combined. Stir in the chocolate chips and pecans, if desired.

Pour the batter into the prepared pan. Bake for 60 to 65 minutes, until deep golden brown and a toothpick inserted comes out clean or with moist crumbs. Cool in the pan on a wire rack for 15 minutes. After 15 minutes, place the cooling rack on top of the cake, hold the sides firmly and invert the pan over the rack. The cake should drop smoothly out of the pan. Tap firmly on the pan with a wooden spoon, if necessary, to free the cake from the pan. Let the cake cool completely.

To make the glaze, combine the chocolate chips and butter in a small glass bowl. Microwave at 50 percent power for 90 seconds. Stir to combine. Microwave an additional 30 seconds at full power and stir again. Microwave for 30 seconds more, if needed, and stir until the chocolate has melted.

Pour the glaze over the cake. The glaze will harden as it cools. Store at room temperature, loosely covered, preferably not airtight. This cake will keep nicely for 2 to 3 days.

Cook's Note: A 10-cup (2400-ml) Bundt pan will also work for this recipe. The cake will simply be more rounded on the bottom after it is removed from the pan.

COCONUT LOVER'S OATMEAL BARS

Yield:
12–16 servings

If you have coconut lovers in your life, this dessert is sure to be a dream come true for them. Chewy, slightly salty, sweet and full of chocolate pieces, these coconut bars are an amazing dessert that requires barely five minutes' effort to get into the oven. This is a fork-required dessert that proves irresistible to any coconut or oatmeal lover!

½ cup (112 g) unsalted butter, melted

½ cup (112 g) packed light brown sugar

1 large egg

1 tsp (5 ml) vanilla extract

2 cups (160 g) old-fashioned oats

1½ cups (125 g) sweetened coconut flakes

½ cup (90 g) dark or semisweet chocolate chips (optional)

½ cup (90 g) white chocolate chips (optional)

½ cup (55 g) finely chopped salted and roasted cashews (optional)

Preheat the oven to 325°F (170°C, or gas mark 3). Lightly grease an 8-inch (20-cm) square pan with butter. In a large mixing bowl, stir together the butter and brown sugar. Add the egg and vanilla and stir until smooth. Stir in the oats and coconut until well combined. Add the chocolate chips and nuts, if desired, and stir again.

Scrape the mixture into the prepared pan and press evenly into the pan. Bake for 25 to 28 minutes, until the coconut is golden and lightly toasted around the edges. Remove from the oven and let cool completely before slicing. Store in an airtight container.

Cook's Notes: This is one time when it really pays to be patient and allow the bars to cool completely before slicing, unless you want to serve them warm with a scoop of ice cream on top for a spectacular dessert.

If you aren't a fan of chocolate or nuts or don't happen to have them in the pantry, I've made these bars numerous times without any of the optional add-ins and I love them every bit as much in their simpler form.

NEVER-FAIL BLONDIES

Yield:
9–12 servings

Blondies are the dessert recipe that everyone needs to have in his or her back pocket. When you combine the texture of a brownie with the deep flavors of the ultimate chocolate chip cookie, you get a rich and chewy treat that everyone loves.

With only six main ingredients, this recipe comes together in minutes with just a bowl and a spoon. Toss in a few handfuls of your favorite add-ins and you'll have these bars ready for the oven before it preheats.

BLONDIES
½ cup (112 g) unsalted butter, melted

1 cup (225 g) packed light brown sugar

1 egg

2 tsp (10 ml) vanilla extract

1 cup (120 g) all-purpose flour*

¼ tsp kosher salt

FAVORITE ADD-IN COMBINATIONS
1 cup (175 g) chocolate chips, any kind

¾ cup (130 g) semisweet chocolate chips + ½ cup (55 g) chopped pecans

¾ cup (130 g) white or dark chocolate chips + ½ cup (70 g) macadamia nuts

¾ cup dark (130 g) chocolate chunks + ½ cup (55 g) chopped walnuts

1 cup (80 g) shredded coconut + 1 cup (175 g) mixed chocolate chips (white, milk, semisweet and dark)

⅔ cup (110 g) caramel bits + ⅔ cup (115 g) semisweet chocolate chips

* GLUTEN-FREE SUBSTITUTION
⅔ cup (98 g) brown rice flour

¼ cup (32 g) tapioca starch

3 tbsp (33 g) potato starch

Preheat the oven to 350°F (180°C, or gas mark 4). Line an 8-inch (20-cm) square pan with parchment paper or line with foil and grease the foil very well.

To make the blondies, in a large bowl, stir together the butter and brown sugar until smooth. Add the egg and vanilla and stir to combine. Stir in the flour and salt, just until combined. Stir in the add-in combination of your choice, reserving a couple of tablespoons (25 g) of the add-ins to sprinkle on top if you'd like.

Scoop the batter into the prepared pan and spread to the sides. Bake for 25 to 28 minutes, until an inserted toothpick has moist crumbs. The blondies should be slightly browned along the edges. Cool in the pan for at least 20 minutes and then lift the blondies out by the paper/foil and set on a wire rack to finish cooling before slicing and storing in an airtight container.

Cook's Notes: This recipe can be doubled to fill a 9 x 13-inch (23 x 33-cm) pan. The doubled recipe will need to be baked for 40 to 45 minutes, until an inserted toothpick has moist crumbs. Slice into 16 to 24 servings.

You can make this recipe in a greased pan without any liner at all. I simply prefer the ease of lifting the bars from the pan by the sides of the parchment or foil and slicing them outside of the pan.

COCONUT LIME ICE CREAM

Yield:
6 servings

Fresh, light and rich all at the same time, this ice cream is truly amazing. I've served it in cones or scooped on top of Lemon Lover's Pound Cake (page 167), and we've eaten it straight out of the freezer with a couple of spoons.

Homemade ice cream is one of my weaknesses. With more than 60 ice cream recipes archived on my Web site, I am a confirmed ice cream addict. It was hard, but I managed to limit myself to just one ice cream recipe in this book, and as far as I'm concerned, this recipe alone would be reason enough to buy an ice cream maker.

½ cup plus 2 tbsp (150 ml) sweetened condensed milk, about 7 oz

2–3 tbsp (12–18 g) lime zest, very finely minced, about 3 large limes

½ cup (120 ml) fresh lime juice, about 5 large limes

1 (14-oz [392-g]) can coconut cream

½ cup (100 g) sugar

⅛ tsp fine sea salt

½ tsp vanilla extract

2 tbsp (30 ml) dark rum (optional)

In a large bowl, whisk together the condensed milk, lime zest and lime juice until smooth. Add the coconut cream, sugar, salt, vanilla and rum, if using, and whisk to combine. Refrigerate for 6 hours or overnight, until well chilled. Pour into your ice cream machine and freeze according to the manufacturer's directions. Transfer to a freezer-safe airtight container and place in the freezer until ready to serve.

Cook's Notes: This recipe specifies coconut cream, not coconut milk. You'll find coconut cream in most grocery stores next to the coconut milk. Although the rum is optional and the small amount might not sound like enough to worry about, it works nicely to deepen the flavor.

You'll need exactly half of a 14-ounce (392-g) can of sweetened condensed milk for this recipe. If you have a kitchen scale, I find it easiest to measure by weight.

The prep time for this recipe is just a few minutes, but a minimum of 6 hours' chill time in the refrigerator is required before churning in order for the ice cream to set.

Acknowledgments

Sean: From my first attempt at biscuits almost twenty years ago, to the final recipes in this book, you have eaten everything. Thanks for trusting that the girl you married really would learn to cook, even when she doubted it herself. You've believed in me from day one and without you this cookbook never would have been written. You are the best husband I could have imagined and I look forward to living life with you every day.

Sam, Ben and Nate: For tasting each recipe and giving your honest opinions, for washing every single dish, for helping clean and tidy the house while I was busy cooking, for making me laugh and smile and pause in my work to marvel at how proud I am of you three. You boys are God's gift to me and I am so happy to be your mom.

Mom: You told me once that my siblings were the greatest gift you would ever give me. I didn't understand that as a child, but as an adult, I couldn't agree more. You've given me a life that riches couldn't buy. You are the best mom I ever could have asked for. Thank you will never be enough.

To all of my siblings: Whether you were one of the first eight kids or you married into our craziness, you've supported, encouraged, tasted, tested and given so much feedback on my food over the years. You've all helped make me the person I am today.

Jenny: For being my biggest cheerleader, for never tiring of hearing a dinner replay, for testing so many recipes, for reminding me to step out of the kitchen occasionally and live life. Your phone calls are highlights of my days.

Miles: For your willingness to taste every single recipe, for the honest feedback and for all the board games you played with the kids while I was working.

Meseidy and Rebecca: For the laughter, the sarcasm, the brainstorming, the advice, the everything. You girls make every day of my life better, just by being the amazing friends you are.

To every single person who tested a recipe: You lovely, wonderful, amazing people helped so much. I can't thank you enough.

To my blogger friends: I couldn't possibly name you all, but you know who you are. You've supported me, cheered me, made me laugh and taught me so much. My life is infinitely better because of the blogging community that surrounds me. You all are rock stars to me.

To my blog readers: I'm so happy to call you my friends. We've cooked and learned together over the years and I can't imagine my life without my little corner of the Internet and each of you.

To the entire team at Page Street, Sarah and Will: You made this book possible, and for that I'm grateful. Thanks for the support, the guidance and the cookbook writing experience that turned out to be more fun than I ever imagined possible.

About the Author

If you had asked her friends and loved ones fifteen years ago, they might have said that Mary Younkin was, perhaps, one of the unlikeliest people to write a cookbook. Thankfully for us all, she combined her love for food and passion for learning. She not only learned to cook, but learned to cook like a pro.

From an avowed hater of dinner prep to a regular meal planner and talented home cook, Mary has truly found her niche in simple home cooking. Her popular recipe blog, Barefeet in the Kitchen, is home to over 1,200 recipes that make cooking from scratch as simple as possible.

A well-respected voice in the world of food blogging, Mary creates recipes that are accessible for both new and experienced home cooks, always with an abundance of flavor. Her first cookbook, *The Weeknight Dinner Cookbook*, is dedicated to her passion for creating family-friendly meals that are easy enough to make on a busy weeknight.

Mary lives in Phoenix, Arizona, with her husband, children and an extensive collection of spatulas and whisks.

Index